MISS AMERICA

The Dream Lives On

A 75-Year Celebration

by Angela Saulino Osborne

Foreword by Heather Whitestone · Introduction by Leonard C. Horn

JACK SMITH
Publisher and Director, Fine Books

BOB SNODGRASS
Publishing Consultant

JOHN FRANK
Photo Editor

VICKI GOLD LEVI
Researcher

JIM THORNTON
Researcher

JEANNE WARREN
Editor

ANITA STUMBO
Design and Typography

Dust Jack Design: Robert Engle Design

Contributing Photographers: John Frank, Sid Schrier, Kathleen Frank, John Maxwell,
Vern Ogrodnek, Al Gold, Nancy Rokos, David Bartley and Andrew Eccles

Select photos courtesy of the: Press of Atlantic City, Hess-Atlantic City Photos, the Vicki Gold Levi Collection,
CP News, the Bettmann Collection, and the Dawn Moiras Collection

Remaining photos courtesy of The Miss America Organization

Original set designs by: Charles Lisanby, pages 2–3, 5, 22–23, 230–231, 232–233, 234–235, 236–237;
Ray Klausen, cover, pages 38–39, 45–47, 115, 166–167, 182, 200–201, gatefold;
Don Shirley, pages 6–7; and Herb Andrews, page 109

Published by Taylor Publishing Company, Dallas, Texas

ISBN: 0-87833-110-7 (General)
ISBN: 0-87833-111-5 (Limited)
ISBN: 0-87833-112-3 (Collectors)

To my husband Bernie
and my daughters Alicia and Rachel,
who fought the dust bunnies and soap suds,
found the grocery store and the refrigerator,
tackled homework and swim meets,
and learned to find lost objects
without asking "Where is . . . ?"
so this book could become a reality.
Thank you for your love, faith and patience.

Contents

foreword

AT THE CLOSE of last year's Miss America Pageant, the shock of winning kept me from immediately appreciating all of the exciting aspects of becoming Miss America. It wasn't until later that I realized not only had I captured the title, but I would serve my term during a landmark year . . . the seventy-fifth anniversary. What an honor. I often think back over seventy-five years of Miss America, in great awe of the legacy of which I am now a part, and with appreciation for what it means to be Miss America in my day and age.

I feel a great sense of pride when I hear young people tell me, "Someday I want to be just like you." A young person who says that to a Miss America today is talking about her life, and is not making a comment about her appearance.

My duty as a Miss America of the nineties is to encourage people with my platform message, "Anything is Possible," and to enhance the quality of life of those who can profit from my experiences. That is my job. A Miss America primarily reflecting glamour, beauty, and perfection is an icon of the past. As a teenager, I was probably considered studious and a hard worker. I didn't run with the popular crowd, or receive many invitations to date. I never took a beauty course or won a homecoming contest. These were not qualities I needed to pursue the Miss America title.

Since infancy, my life has demanded a constant commitment to overcoming obstacles; this has created my desire to open new doors, for others as well as myself. It's one of life's great ironies that a perceived weakness — being profoundly deaf — did so much to make me a stronger person. People seem to want to hear about my disability and how a negative can be turned into a positive. I think they would feel differently about me if I were able to say, "I've had the perfect life."

This is why I say that becoming a Miss America these days is an awesome responsibility and a great honor. It means so much more than having a nice appearance, and even a polished talent. In short, becoming Miss America means that you have lived your life well. It means you are perceived as having achieved a well-rounded sense of discipline, and more importantly, that you have a message. It means the panel which selected you believes your message is credible and formidable enough to the improve the quality of life of your fellow Americans.

Therefore I am honored to be a Miss America during the nineties, during a time when Miss America has progressed into a position of such incredible impact. That sense of honor combines with my pride in being part of the legacy of Miss America, to be part of such an enduring piece of American history. As my name becomes part of the nostalgia, I look forward to the future — to watch as new Miss Americas are elected and given the chance to have even greater impact on each new generation.

— HEATHER WHITESTONE
MISS AMERICA 1995

prologue

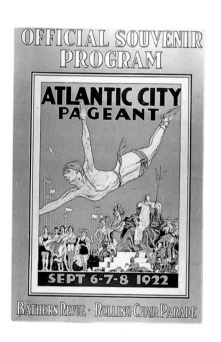

THE YEAR IS 1920. America is emerging from the memory of World War One. Women have the right to vote. Prohibition is the law of the land. Radio is used for the first time to broadcast the results of a presidential election. And in Southern New Jersey, a sleepy resort community looks for a way to extend its summer season beyond Labor Day.

Along the East Coast, September offers the loveliest weather of the year. Ironically, this is the same month families pack up, wash the sand off their souvenir sea shells, and trade summer clothes for school clothes. For the "shore," as the New Jersey Coast is called, has always been a family vacation spot. Its beaches are left to the seagulls and sand crabs the day after Labor Day — the traditional start of the new school year.

That year, the Atlantic City's Business Men's League sponsors a Fall Frolic in hopes of extending the shore's tourist season. The famous Atlantic City Rolling Chairs, those wicker hand-wheeled vehicles that invoke an exotic hint of the Far East and are a boardwalk fixture to this day, are showcased in an hour-long parade down Atlantic Avenue. Billed as the International Rolling Chair Pageant, the parade is led by a beautiful woman dressed in flowing white robes. She is called, simply, "Peace." Unknown to all, she is the precursor of Miss America.

While the Fall Frolic is only moderately successful in increasing patronage of the resort, the potential of extending the season past Labor Day with some sort of special event is clear. But what kind of event? Asbury Park, about sixty miles up the coast, has its famous Baby Parade. As exotic as they might be, rolling chairs, even when bedecked in flowers and crepe paper, can't compete with darling cherubs dressed in diapers and ribbons.

Somehow Atlantic City must put its assets together in an original and exciting way. In addition to its rolling chairs, it has a unique boardwalk,

beautiful beaches, a string of lovely hotels, and the entertaining Steel Pier. An extraordinary event to draw the crowds — that's the answer.

In 1921, a newly formed committee suggests a Bathing Beauty Review. The idea is simple: combine the need to expand the circulation of area newspapers with the need to attract people to the resort. The papers will run a contest, urging readers to submit pictures of beautiful young women. Each participating newspaper will send their winning entry to Atlantic City, where the "fairest" of them will be crowned.

The first Pageant is called a "National Beauty Tournament." Herb Test, a reporter for the *Atlantic City Press* hired to handle publicity for the revue, says "and we'll call her 'Miss America.'"

Thus, an American tradition is born.

acknowledgments

I DEEPLY APPRECIATE the assistance given to me by the staff of The Miss America Organization in developing this book. Special thanks to Miss America's CEO Leonard C. Horn; Karen Aarons, who provided a great deal of background information and history on the Pageant; Leonard Hill, for explaining the judging process so thoroughly; Jayne Bray and Marilyn Feehan, who gave me an insider's look at the hostess committee in action; and Carol Plum-Ucci and Bill Caligari of the Miss America Organization. My heartfelt thanks to Jim Thornton of the Miss America Organization, who gave so much, so willingly, to this project. His meticulous research, patience, and encyclopedic knowledge of the Miss America Pageant helped make this book possible. And, course, I want to thank all the Miss Americas who shared their memories with me.

I am grateful for the encouragement I received from John L. Koushouris, my former boss and the television producer of the Miss America Pageant for thirty-one years. His emotional support kept me focused, and his invaluable information about the early days of televising the Pageant gave shape to the book.

Anita Stumbo deserves recognition for approaching Taylor Publishing Company with the idea for a book commemorating Miss America's seventy-fifth anniversary... and for her design of the book, which reflects the elegance and style for which the Pageant is known.

I'm also very grateful to my editor, Jeanne Warren, who smoothed out the rough spots and helped keep this project moving.

Finally, my special thanks to Bob Snodgrass of Taylor Publishing for his unflagging support and direction in developing this project, and his dogged insistence that I could make this book a reality.

—A.O.

introduction

MERELY READING THE WORDS, "seventy-five years of life," does not begin to convey the full meaning, nor the durability, of Miss America. It is only when you stop to realize the major events and changes in the world since she was "born" in 1921 that you begin to appreciate the profound appeal that Miss America has had to millions and millions of people throughout the decades of the twentieth century.

Certainly, there have been detractors; but, Miss America must have done something right to have endured for seventy-five years. Just think. From the time that Miss America was first crowned on the boardwalk as a publicity gimmick for Atlantic City . . . to the crowning of Heather Whitestone, Miss America 1995 . . . we have seen fourteen United States Presidents, the Great Depression, World War II, the Korean War, the Vietnam War. We have witnessed the advent of television, the development of commercial flying, the first man to walk on the moon. We have survived major socioeconomic changes in society. The first Miss America broadcast came at a time when televisions were a novelty to most people — to such an extent that they would sit and stare at test patterns. Today, the average household occupies itself with thirty-five stations plus VHS programming as opposed to the one or two channels that aired during the fifties. Yet, Miss America still thrives as a major, top-rated television special every September.

What is the spell Miss America has cast over this country for three-quarters of the twentieth century? Why do millions of people still look upon her as a role model? Why do Americans still look forward to seeing her crowned on a Saturday night in September? Everybody has an opinion about Miss America: who she is, who she should be, who and what she should represent, and, indeed, whether she should even continue to exist.

Today, Miss America is a dynamic, relevant, young role model. She is an activist, and she uses her God-given abilities, together with her education, to place the Miss America spotlight and celebrity on significant social issues. She is ambitious, she believes in the pursuit of higher education. Over the years, the scholarships bearing her title have brought education and opportunity to thousands of women.

People of all ages identify with Miss America and try to emulate her — what she does, what she says. And through the vast organization supporting her, Miss America provides significant benefits to society.

She started humbly. She grew and adjusted throughout the various chapters of twentieth century history. Miss America has not only survived, but she has emerged as a person of considerable influence and relevancy. Even the toughest of critics would agree that her endurance is noteworthy.

This, then, is her story.

— **LEONARD C. HORN**
President and CEO
The Miss America Organization

Chapter One

"...and the new Miss America is..."

Standing on that stage waiting for the announcement
of the top ten, you tell yourself that just making it to
Atlantic City is a marvelous achievement... but once
you know you are one of the top ten that's no longer
enough... now that the crown is within reach, you
want to win that crown, and you only want to win.

— SUSAN POWELL
MISS AMERICA 1981

Lights... cameras...

CAVERNOUS. That's the only way to describe the inside of the Convention Center in Atlantic City. Thirteen stories soar to an arched roof, 675 feet long by 351 feet wide. Previously the site of indoor football games, horse races, ice shows, wrestling matches, prize fights, concerts, and ice hockey, tonight Convention Center resembles not so much an arena as a fairyland, a place where dreams come true.

This night, fifty of the country's loveliest, most talented, most dedicated young women capture America's attention on one of the largest stages in the world. Tonight 15,000 people sit on metal bleachers in a semicircle around that famed runway, anxiously waiting as nine television cameras poise to deliver Miss America into millions of American homes.

CONVENTION CENTER — ATLANTIC CITY

Opening night jitters disappear
as all fifty contestants joyfully
participate in the opening
production number.

The stage manager's voice booms over the loudspeakers.

"Five minutes to air . . . four minutes . . . three minutes . . . one
minute . . . thirty seconds . . . ten seconds!" The house reverberates
with the audience countdown of the remaining seconds: "Five, four,
three, two, one!" At 9:00 P.M. on September 17, 1994, the Miss
America Pageant is on the air!

The houselights dim. Spotlights bathe the stage in brilliance, and
"Luck Be A Lady Tonight" rings out from the orchestra. The crowd roars as
fifty Miss America contestants dance and sing their way through the opening
production number. Each contestant, in turn, walks to the microphone and
announces her name to wild cheers from her supporters.

The stage goes dark as the production number ends. The millions watching at home see a commercial, but those in the audience are caught up in a
frenzy. The houselights play over members of the audience, who cheer and
call out the names of their favorites. To the audience, the show doesn't start
until the top ten are announced. The few moments left to wait move at a
snail's pace for those in Convention Center.

Finally, at 9:20, the top ten contestants are announced: Kansas, Ohio, New Jersey, Virginia, Indiana, Georgia, Alabama, Mississippi, Texas and Montana! Forty others — after months of competing in local and state pageants — know they will never be Miss America, but for these finalists the competition is just beginning. Ten smiles light up the stage to thunderous applause.

Standing on Convention Center's enormous stage, under the glare of thousands of watts of electricity, dwarfed by oversized sets, the contestants appear doll-like and vulnerable to the live audience. But to millions watching at home they are larger than life, radiating energy, style, talent, and composure.

All fifty contestants participate in every production number. Those no longer in the running still gamely dance and smile their way through the swimsuit competition to the music of the Beach Boys. Contestants frolic barefoot through this beach scene. That's right — for the first time in Pageant history, these contestants compete sans high heels . . . a big moment in itself! Then the ten finalists, in turn, break away from the dancers, and with a beach

The moment everyone is waiting for — the top ten contestants are: Miss Kansas, Miss Ohio, Miss New Jersey, Miss Virginia, Miss Indiana, Miss Georgia, Miss Alabama, Miss Mississippi, Miss Texas, Miss Montana

Contestants smile their way through the swimsuit production number and competition — and no one is wearing high heels!

Judges — model Cheryl Tiegs, Olympic gold medalist Dan Jansen and Miss America 1981 Susan Powell — pay close attention to the proceedings. Behind them are auditors from Price Waterhouse.

Right (clockwise): Miss Kansas, Trisha Schaffer; Miss Ohio, Lea Mack; Miss New Jersey, Jennifer Makris; Miss Virginia, Cullen Johnson; Miss Indiana, Tiffany Storm; Miss Georgia, Andrea Krahn.

towel rakishly tossed over one shoulder, strut and turn in front of the judges. Though cleverly integrated into the production number, looking good in a swimsuit is still a clear part of this competition. The more things change . . .

The music ends and the curtain closes; the contestants have made it through the first phase of competition. Still ahead is the very tough talent portion of the show, and the ever-telling on-stage interview.

The first to brave the stage alone is Miss Kansas, Trisha Schaffer, holding the crowd spellbound with a pop vocal, "Orange Colored Sky." Next is Miss Ohio, Lea Mack, offering a change of pace with a semiclassical song. Miss New Jersey, Jennifer Makris, sings a sultry rendition of "The Man That Got Away," and Miss Virginia, Cullen Johnson, dazzles the crowd with her brilliant interpretation of Beethoven's "Sonata Pathetique" at the piano. Miss Indiana, Tiffany Storm, follows, bringing pop music back to the stage.

Five down, five to go. Even at the most celebrated Broadway show it would be difficult to sit through ten talent performances that are not part of an integrated story or score. The talent portion of the competition takes endurance — from the audience as well as the performers; however, the commercial

breaks allow the home viewers and the live audience to take a breather, and to begin lining up their favorites.

Back on the air, Miss Georgia, Andrea Krahn, takes command of the stage with her version of the Patsy Cline country hit, "I Fall To Pieces." Then it's Miss Alabama's turn. Heather Whitestone is a vision in white tulle. She wows the crowd with her graceful classical ballet. Earlier in the week, during preliminary judging, she was a winner in both the swimsuit and talent contests. She's grabbed the audience, whose deafening chant, "Hea-ther . . . Hea-ther . . ." fills the auditorium. She's clearly a finalist.

Heather is a hard act to follow, but Miss Mississippi, Rebecca Blouin, bravely faces the cameras with a lovely classical vocal. Miss Texas, Arian Archer, sails through another pop vocal with ease and style, and finally Miss Montana, Yvonne Dehner, ends the talent portion of the competition with the semiclassical vocal, "One Kiss."

One and one-half hours have passed . . . one hour to go.

The current Miss America walks the runway for the last time to a standing ovation, and presents the 1994 Woman of Achievement Award. The competition resumes with all ten contestants in the evening wear portion of the show, poised and dazzling, but with the most difficult competition still ahead.

After another commercial break, the winners of the Bert Parks' Talent Scholarships are announced. Then, at last, comes the moment everyone has been waiting for — the naming of the five finalists. Miss Georgia, Miss Alabama, Miss New Jersey, Miss Virginia, and Miss Indiana are the final hopefuls. There are alternately moans and cheers as these five states come closer to their dream, while five others know they will not produce a Miss America this year.

Right: Miss Alabama, Heather Whitestone

Below L–R: Miss Mississippi, Rebecca Blouin; Miss Texas, Arian Archer; Miss Montana, Yvonne Dehner.

The night's biggest challenge is at hand for the five finalists, as each is asked a question pertaining to her platform. Exuding confidence and self-assurance, the young women belie the nervousness they each feel. The show continues with more musical divertissements while the final scores are tallied. On stage, five beautiful women clutch each other's hands as they await the announcement that will change one of their lives forever.

An assistant hands the envelope to the host, and an eerie silence fills the vast auditorium. The results are: Fourth Runner-Up, Miss Indiana; Third, Miss Georgia; Second, Miss New Jersey; and First Runner-Up, Miss Virginia. Miss Alabama, who can't hear the announcement, is unaware of the results.

The top five finalists take center stage: Miss Georgia, Miss Alabama, Miss New Jersey, Miss Virginia, Miss Indiana. Another challenge ahead for each of them is the interview competition.

Left: Miss America 1994, Kimberly Aiken, walks the runway for the last time.

First Runner-Up Miss Virginia, Cullen Johnson says, "It's you!" to Heather Whitestone.

A jubilant Heather is congratulated by Miss Indiana and Miss Mississippi.

Right: Miss America 1994, Kimberly Aiken, crowns her successor, Miss America 1995, Heather Whitestone.

"There She Is, Miss America"
© Bernie Wayne. Reprinted by permission.

Miss Virginia mouths the words "It's you!" and Miss Alabama gasps in delight.

Heather Whitestone regains her composure and begins her walk down the famous 125-foot runway. She waves at the cheering audience as photographers surge forward to capture the scene and hundreds of flashes from audience cameras send waves of light throughout the arena.

History has been made this night. Miss America, always intelligent, beautiful, talented and charming, for the first time is also deaf. She will be a special inspiration to people around the globe. The audience sings along with hosts Regis Philbin and Kathie Lee Gifford to the song that has carved itself into American folklore:

"There she is, Miss America . . .
There she is, your ideal. . . ."

And there she is, Miss America 1995, Heather Whitestone — America's ideal!

LEE MERIWETHER
MISS AMERICA 1955

CAROLYN SAPP
MISS AMERICA 1992

PHYLLIS GEORGE
MISS AMERICA 1971

PAMELA ELDRED
MISS AMERICA 1970

KYLENE BARKER
MISS AMERICA 1979

CHERYL PREWITT
MISS AMERICA 1980

SUSAN POWELL
MISS AMERICA 1981

SUSAN AKIN
MISS AMERICA 1986

EXCLUSIVE PAG
PHOTO
FRED HE
166 SOUTH
ATLANT

BER 5th to 10th, 1960 — CONVENTION HALL, ATLANTIC CITY, N

MISS AMERICA PAGEANT — SEPTEMI

W I N N I N G   M O M E N T S

Gretchen Carlson is crowned Miss America 1989 by Kaye Lani Rae Rafko,
Miss America 1988, as the tradition continues.

A Tradition Is Born

For a few hours on a Saturday night in September people can escape to a world of positive images of young Americans. Maybe that's why the Pageant has endured. It gives us hope.

— KAREN AARONS
Executive Vice President
The Miss America Organization

Tradition

LET'S FACE IT. The Miss America Pageant isn't up there with the Fourth of July or Thanksgiving when it comes to celebrating American traditions. Or is it? Just as surely as we can expect fireworks on Independence Day and phone calls home the fourth Thursday of every November, we can expect to celebrate the Miss America Pageant two weeks after Labor Day, every September.

About the time Jersey shore residents are cleaning up after an either wildly successful or disastrous summer (depending on whether nature decided to hit them with a few major storms or bless them with glorious sunshine), when the shore birds finally have the beaches to themselves, one place on the

(Previous page)
The nine finalists in 1921: (L–R) Miss New York, Virginia Lee; Miss Pittsburgh, Thelma Matthews; Miss Washington, D.C., Margaret Gorman; Miss Camden, Kathryn Gearon; Miss Newark, Margaret Bates; Miss Ocean City, Hazel Harris; Miss Harrisburg, Emma Pharo; Miss Atlantic City, Ethel Charles; and Miss Philadelphia, Nellie Orr.

MARGARET GORMAN — MISS AMERICA 1921

A seventy-five year tradition begins in Atlantic City. Originally known as
"The Miss Inter-City Beauty Contest," The Miss America Pageant went on to capture the heart of America.

Jersey shore turns itself inside out to accommodate thousands of visitors who cram its hotels and famous boardwalk to be part of the excitement of the Miss America Pageant.

"Whether they hate it or love it, millions of people can't resist it — it's part of our tradition, and people love tradition," says Leonard C. Horn. Horn, who began volunteering for the Pageant in 1963 and is now its CEO and president, adds, "We must be doing something right, or we would not have endured for seventy-five years." Pressed to explain why the Pageant has endured, he says, "Ask the public — they are the ones who made us a part of American culture."

One thing is sure. Creating an American tradition or cultural phenomenon was the last thing H. Conrad Eckholm, owner of the Monticello Hotel in Atlantic City had in mind in 1920 when he urged the Business Men's League in Atlantic City to sponsor a "Fall Frolic" to take place in late September.

That's the best time at the Jersey shore. Summer's prevalent jellyfish and ravenous green flies have all but disappeared. The weather is balmy without being hot, and the ocean is the temperature of a tepid bath. Since most tourists usually rejoin their real lives after Labor Day, this glorious season is lost to them. Eckholm and other Atlantic City businessmen hope their "Fall Frolic" will change that.

Three hundred and fifty gaily decorated rolling chairs were pushed along the parade route by three hundred and fifty able-bodied men, whose abilities to participate in the festivities depended on muscle power, not the power to charm the cheering crowds. The charm belonged to the young "maidens" who sat in those rolling chairs and graced the parade with their smiles and beauty. Led by Miss Ernestine Cremona, who was dressed in flowing white robes and represented "Peace," the parade was a success.

Although local newspapers described the event as a "glittering spectacle" and its audience as an "admiring throng," Atlantic City's businessmen were well aware they had to compete with similar events that took place in other resorts along New Jersey's 139-mile coastline. The rolling chair pageant wasn't enough, but the men knew they were on to something, so they decided to try again the following year.

Atlantic City needed an attraction, and Atlantic City area newspapers needed to increase circulation. Voila! A perfect opportunity for an enduring partnership! During the winter of 1921, Harry Finley, an Atlantic City newspaperman, attended a meeting of circulation managers who were seeking ways to increase circulation of their respective newspapers and he had a brainstorm! Why not run a popularity contest in each of the various cities to select the most popular young lady? The winners of the newspaper contests would then gather in Atlantic City where they would take part in that city's September pageant and where the most beautiful entrant would receive a trophy. The idea was presented to Sam Leeds, president of the Chamber of

miss america speaks

Commerce. It was accepted and the hotelmen's association agreed to entertain the respective young ladies for the week following Labor Day.

On September 3, 1921, in a page one article, *The Atlantic City Daily Press* announced the availability of tickets for the "Atlantic City Pageant." The event was conceived as a two-day series of attractions which included: the Inter-City Beauty Contest, the Frolique of Neptune, the Bathers' Revue, a Baby Parade, the Rolling Chair Parade, and admission to the Governor's Ball on the Steel Pier.

The contestants were divided into several classes: "Professional Beauties" (actresses, showgirls, models), "Civic Beauties" (amateurs), and "Inter-City Beauties" (entrants in the newspaper contest). In that first pageant, contestants were judged in numerous events, including the Rolling Chair Parade and the Bathers' Revue, before the winners of those events became the finalists — a precursor to today's system, in which contestants compete in a variety of categories before going to head-to-head in a final competition.

The article announced a first place prize of $100.00 to the winner of the Inter-City Beauty Contest. Silver cups and gold metals would be awarded independently for Comic Costumes, Bathers' Revue, Amateur Beauties, Professional Beauties, Baby Parade and Rolling Chairs.

Miss Pittsburgh smiles at the crowd thronging the boardwalk during the 1921 rolling chair parade.

Hudson Maxim, as King Neptune, is surrounded by his court of twenty beauties and twenty "slaves" at the landing of the Yacht Club in 1921. Their arrival kicked off the festivities at the first Miss America Competition.

Retired and widowed for five years, Marilyn resides in Mount Dora, Florida, and enjoys keeping active.

66

There has been no negative impact for me being Miss America. It has opened doors for me, given me the experience of making appearances around the country, and helped me to gain confidence. I believe the Pageant has endured because its standards are very high, and all those wonderful volunteers work so hard to keep it that way.

99

Marilyn Meseke with son Michael Hume and husband Ben Rogers.

miss america speaks

In 1923 swimsuits were still quite modest. Here, a contestant wears a skirted dress over pants with long stockings.

In coming up with the title "Miss America," Herb Test, a reporter for the *Atlantic City Daily Press,* could not have known he had coined a phrase that would become as identifiably American as the Statue of Liberty. He was only thinking of increasing the circulation of the area's newspapers, while the local businessmen behind the scheme dreamed of fattening their wallets.

A list of rules in the same paper warned that for the "Bathers' Revue" portion of the pageant, "judges will act as censors, the Board of Censors reserve the right to reject any entry they deem objectionable and all entrants must *positively* be attired in bathing costumes."

This seeming contradiction of purpose was nothing new to the guardians of Atlantic City. This resort, whose main attraction was its beaches certainly couldn't tell its tourists *not* to wear bathing costumes, but it had laws on the books which determined just how much uncovered skin could be displayed in public.

In 1921, the *New York Times* reported that one bather risked jail by rolling her stockings down and baring her knees. Louise Rosine, 39, a novelist, declared: "It's none of the city's darn business whether I roll 'em up or down."

Margaret Gorman, Miss America 1921, accepts the key to Atlantic City from King Neptune, marking the official kickoff of the 1922 Pageant festivities.

The article further reported that Rosine assaulted the cop who attempted to arrest her and landed in jail.

There it was — right at the beginning. The makings of the conflict that has plagued the Pageant: an absolute requirement that contestants be attired in bathing costumes and be judged in "beauty and form," while maintaining an air of modesty. No young lady would disgrace this "Graceful Dowager" of the Jersey Shore, Atlantic City. The board of censors would see to that!

This contradiction in terms persists. For years, Pageant officials have threatened to eliminate the swimsuit competition altogether, and most recently the Pageant has been referring to that part of the show as "excellence in physical fitness," thereby attempting to remove all vestiges of its original "bathing beauty" image.

This embarrassment over bathing suit best manifested itself in 1946 when Pageant Director Lenora Slaughter banned the words "bathing suit" from Pageant vocabulary. "We will refer to that part of the Pageant as the swimsuit competition," she ordered.

The wearing of swimsuits not only was a conundrum for Pageant officials; for years its been a source of bewilderment and panic for contestants. In the

Left: By the late 1930s the demure bathing costumes of the twenties were just a memory, as evidenced by Marilyn Meseke, Miss America 1938, who poses in a shimmering one piece suit.

Middle: Throughout the thirties and forties, contestants like Marilyn Buferd, Miss America 1946, sometimes wore two-piece suits and posed with the same sweet sexiness evoked by Betty Grable's famous pin-up picture of World War II.

Below: Sashed contestants sashay in sand and sun in 1958.

thirties and forties contestants sometimes wore two-piece suits, and unabashedly posed in their suits with the same sweet sexiness that was evoked in Betty Grable's famous pinup picture of World War II.

Sometime in the sixties, all contestants were required to wear one-piece suits with a paneled front. Long after that look was out of style, the requirement continued, and contestants would frantically search stores for the mandated suit because there just weren't that many of them around. It wasn't until 1970 that Phyllis George competed in a bright yellow, more fashionable, non-panel suit. But in 1921, The "Inter-City Beauty Contest" was what it was — a beauty contest.

Bathing suits notwithstanding, right from its inception the Pageant has attempted to cloak itself in respectability. An article in the *Atlantic City Daily Press* that first year proclaimed, "Most of the social leaders of the country now in the resort attended the festivities," and the caption under the picture of Miss Atlantic City, Ethel Charles noted, "She has just returned from taking an invitation to President and Mrs. Harding to come to Atlantic City for the Pageant on Wednesday and Thursday."

On September 6, 1921, the *Daily Press* headlined: "Pageant Beauties arrive today," and referred to the arriving contestants as "beauty maids." The next day, *Press* headlines read, "Curtain Rolls Back Today on Big Pageant — Beauties Captivate Great Throngs" and "Neptune to Make Spectacular Landing on Beach Near Million Dollar Pier."

Indeed, it was "King Neptune," not Bert Parks, who presented the first award to a "Miss America" (although at the time the winner was simply called "The Miss Inter-City Beauty Contest Winner").

"King Neptune," a role played by Hudson Maxim, the inventor of smokeless gunpowder, came ashore on a barge bedecked with flowers with a "court of mermaids," wearing a seaweed robe and a long white beard that flowed in the shore breeze.

His arrival was heralded in the *Daily Press* with the headline: "Neptune Arrives, Waves Magic Trident, and Super Carnival Grips the Resort." The article continued: "Emerging from his marine Kingdom here yesterday morning . . . the Ruler of the Seas, with one majestic sweep of his trident, relegated business and other earthly cares to the background, turning Atlantic City into a super carnival center . . . His Majesty of the Waves disembarked from his shell barge with his court of mermaids."

It was quite a sight. Airplanes showered the scene with confetti, grand yachts, their decks jammed with affluent spectators, surrounded Neptune's barge, deck guns boomed their salute, "while whistles, sirens, church bells, and other noisemakers chorused in a bedlam of greeting from every part of the resort." The Press didn't stint on adjectives: "King Neptune". . ."Ruler of the Sea". . ."His Majesty of the Waves". . ."King of the Fishes". . ."His Bosship

Paneled suits and high heels were *de rigueur* in the late fifties and sixties. Miss Maryland, Margaret Mackie; Miss West Virginia, Judith Shoup; and Miss Virginia, Sydney Lewis wave to the cameras in 1969. Though upswept hair was not required, it was clearly a favorite style among contestants.

FRANCES MARIE BURKE
MISS AMERICA 1940

Married forty-nine years to Lawrence Kenney, Frances Burke is the mother of four children, and grandmother of five girls and five boys who range in age from two weeks to thirteen years. A volunteer for many years at the St. Francis Country House nursing home in Philadelphia, she also was very active in the PTA while her children were attending school.

99

The Pageant was the highlight of my young life. The honor of being Miss America launched a successful modeling career, gave a jump-start to my self-esteem, and enabled me to meet many wonderful people along the way. My chaperone in Atlantic City was Ruth Bacharach, and we still see each other quite often. The modeling was fun and exciting and it eventually took me to Hollywood. However, the desire to be near my family in Philadelphia and to settle down and raise my own family took priority over a movie career, and it was the best decision I could have made. In the '40s and '50s the Pageant was, for the most part, a beauty contest. I believe it has endured because it has evolved into something more as the emphasis changed to qualities such as talent, education, intelligence, and social responsibility. I applaud the decision to eliminate the high heels in the swimsuit competition, and I'll always be proud to have been a part of an American Dream.

99

of the Seas," were just a few of the nautical names bestowed on Hudson Maxim, the octogenarian businessman who gamely led the celebration. It was clear he thoroughly enjoyed this role — after all, not many businessmen enter show biz at age 81.

The next day, headlines proclaimed, "Miss Washington Carries away Golden Mermaid trophy . . . Capital beauty lands principal trophy of Pageant and Sweeps Boards as Inter-City and Bathers' Revue Queen." More blazing headlines proclaimed that "Beauty and Grace Reign Supreme as Merry Mermaids Revel in One Piece Bathing Suits Before Great Gallery Along The Beach." Beneath the headlines were pictures of the contestants wearing their famous (or infamous) "bathing costumes."

So there they were — just nine young women representing only three states and the District of Columbia. New Jersey gave us Miss Camden, Kathryn Gearon; Miss Ocean City, Hazel Harris; Miss Newark, Margaret Bates; and Miss Atlantic City, Ethel Charles. Pennsylvania's beauties were, Miss Pittsburgh, Thelma Matthews; Miss Harrisburg, Emma Pharo; and Miss Philadelphia, Nellie Orr. Miss New York was Virginia Lee. The entrant from the furthest distance from the "shore" was Miss Washington, D.C., Margaret Gorman. To eliminate charges of local favoritism, Miss Atlantic City dropped out, leaving just eight to compete.

That's all there was to it. Eight young women wearing "bathing costumes," participating in a two-day gala. No doubt about it — though the extravaganza included everything the resort could throw at the crowd, from darling babies to parades to a society ball, it was the "bathing beauties" wearing knee-length dresses and long stockings, complete with hats and bathing shoes, that captivated the crowds.

From newspaper publicity stunt to full-blown glamour event, the Pageant's earliest years evolved into something no one could foretell — an American tradition.

Frances Burke and husband Lawrence Kenney and five of their ten grandchildren.

miss america speaks

BeBe Shopp
Miss America 1948

Chapter Three

There She Was...

Miss America represents the highest ideals. She is a real combination of beauty, grace, and intelligence, artistic and refined. She is a type which the American Girl might well emulate.

— FREDERICK HICKMAN
*President Atlantic City
Chamber of Commerce 1926*

Ideal

THERE SHE WAS . . . sixteen-year-old Margaret Gorman from Washington, D.C., who sent in her picture to a local newspaper and found herself named the most beautiful "maid" in the country. Her trophy was a specially designed golden mermaid consisting of a black teakwood base, with a series of gold seashells around a golden mermaid lying on a real piece of granite rock.

The model for the mermaid was Margaret Katherine Heavens, a teenager who was a dancer with a local dance school troupe. Her daughter, Dawn Morias, remembers the story of how it all happened. "My mother was a beautiful teenage dancer and model. The Pageant had a nautical theme when it began and my grandmother had the idea that a golden mermaid, with my mother as the model, would be a lovely trophy," she says. Pageant officials agreed.

LOIS DELANDER — MISS AMERICA 1927

Originally, the winner was to keep the trophy if she won the title three years in a row, but after a few years, the rules changed, the trophy was kept by the reigning queen, and new prizes were issued.

During the first years of the Pageant, the Golden Mermaid was the first float in the Boardwalk parade, and was the advertising symbol of the Pageant. Margaret Heavens, who later became a Ziegfield Girl and worked in the theater and in films, led the Parade for seven years, returning from wherever she was working to participate in the event.

Because only a few trophies were made, they are very rare. Pageant officials only recently were able to track down one of the original Golden Mermaids and still are searching for others that might be stored in family attics or basements.

Another prize was a two-foot tall silver urn. In a newspaper interview following the first Pageant, Gorman said that her prizes were "very beautiful" and she was "very proud of them." "When I arrive in Washington I am going to carry them under my arms and let the people there see them," she said. Although "there were a bunch of people at the station to meet me, and all that foolishness," fame quickly faded away. For the rest of the year at Western High School, Margaret Gorman settled into the routine of an ordinary schoolgirl.

For the first Miss America, there were no sponsor tours, no ribbon cuttings, no Hollywood offers, and no college scholarships. She went on with her life, eventually became Mrs. Victor Cahill, and still lives in Washington, D.C. In a 1980 interview she said, "I never cared to be Miss America. It wasn't my idea. I am so bored by it all. I really want to forget the whole thing."

While little Margaret Gorman's life was unaffected by her triumph, the businessmen in Atlantic City accomplished their goals. The crowds came, the crowds stayed, and the crowds spent money. Recognizing a good thing when they saw it, these businessmen decided to follow up with a bigger and better event the following year. Pageant director Harry Godshall immediately wrote letters to the most prominent newspapers in every city in the country. It was a public relations gold mine, prompting thousands of words of free publicity in newspapers across America.

The letters touched a nerve. The public was intrigued with the idea and the following year newspapers announced "Beauties representing fifty-eight cities arrived by train, plane, and auto from the East, Pacific Coast, the North, the South, and Canada."

Encouraged by the response, the city, which had tentatively chipped in $1,000 in 1921, upped its appropriation to $12,500 in 1922, and the whole budget almost doubled from $27,000 to $51,000. The money was used to throw an even more fabulous party than the one held the year before. Blasting cannons and blazing fireworks erupted as King Neptune rolled in from the sea on an elaborately decorated barge surrounded by his court of beauties.

miss america speaks

Margaret Heavens represents the Golden Mermaid on a float during the boardwalk parade.

The Golden Mermaid trophy

Newspapers reported: "A shower of scentless flowers was hurled at the old sea king by the sixty or more inter-city beauties and by thousands of spectators who swarmed about them."

Margaret Gorman gallantly defended her crown and was a crowd favorite, but Miss Columbus, sixteen-year-old Mary Catherine Campbell, captured the title before a crowd of 250,000 cheering spectators. Judges looked for "poise as well as facial features," as the contestants competed in bathing suits, and afternoon and evening dresses.

Once again, Pageant officials assumed the role of arbitrator in matters of morals. Bobbed hair was becoming fashionable at the time, and the sight of women emerging from beauty shops with boyish bobbed hair prompted a national debate on the subject. Newspapers reported that "only three of the Inter-City Beauty Contestants had bobbed hair." Pageant rules, which seem to bend or change according to the issue at hand, insisted on "natural beauty," meaning that bobbed hair disqualified or handicapped its wearer. This point of contention was an omen of the controversies that would plague the Pageant throughout its history.

The issue prompted an editorial in the September 10, 1922, *New York Times* which rallied in favor of "enthusiastic feminists who are trying to remove all the disabilities of the fair sex," and called the rule an obvious

BESS MYERSON
MISS AMERICA 1945

After winning the crown, Bess Myerson enjoyed a long career as a television personality, writer, lecturer, and public advocate. She served as Commissioner of Consumer Affairs and of Cultural Affairs in New York City, and was a presidential appointee for Presidents Ford and Carter, dealing with the issues of mental health and world hunger.

Today, Myerson lives in New York City where she is actively involved with the Jewish Anti-Defamation League, and the Jewish Guild for the Blind, among many other charitable causes. Myerson recently established the Myerson Journalism Award; this will go to the winners of an annual essay contest focusing on interfaith and multi-cultural understanding through journalistic excellence in campus student newspapers. The award is administered under the auspices of the Anti-Defamation League.

Daughter Barra Grant and granddaughter Samantha Kate Reilly live in California where Barra is a film and play writer. A cancer and stroke survivor, Myerson volunteers time working with SHARE, a support group for women cancer patients, and says, "their gratitude is better than any applause."

66

I knew that I would carry the title of Miss America for the rest of my life. After the war when we all learned about the Holocaust, I knew I had to use my celebrity to bring dignity to myself and my people. That's when I began speaking up against bigotry and racial discrimination. Everything comes full circle; in 1945 I created a 'platform' for myself, and today having a platform issue is part of Pageant requirements. Everyone needs to look up to someone at some time and if at a certain point in a young girl's life that person is Miss America, well, that can't be bad.

99

miss america speaks

double standard. "Objection to bobbed hair is legitimate enough in Mr. Hudson Maxim, for he practices the worship of 'natural beauty' himself. His beard grows long as Nature made it and floats in the wind like the Star Spangled Banner. But how can an artist or magazine illustrator who voluntarily endures the daily labor of shaving to make himself more beautiful in his own eyes object to the unnatural beauty of a girl who bobs her hair and thereby saves time and trouble?" The editorial went on to chastise the judging process, saying that inasmuch as the girls compete in evening gowns, afternoon frocks, and bathing suits, "The art of the costumer may have as much to do with the result."

The first Atlantic City Pageant coincided with a time in history when women's roles were expanding from the confines of the home. Physical exercise and swimming were becoming acceptable for women as well as men, and the decade was influenced by the young with its modern approach to manners and morals.

Women not only were emerging from "bathing machines" (beach tents in which women changed into bathing attire, and then were pulled, tent and all, into the water to enjoy the benefits of the salt water), they also were emerging from heavy corsets that emphasized a full bust and round hips, and ankle-length skirts that inhibited their mobility.

Margaret Gorman won the first Miss America title wearing a knee length "bathing costume" with long stockings and bathing shoes. It wasn't long before women, having enjoyed the freedom of movement in street wear, were wearing one-piece or two-piece maillots, a style that previously was worn only by men.

The maillot was the problem. Unstructured, braless, usually made of wool which clung to the body when wet, Victorian by today's standards, those early swimsuits revealed the body in a very sexy way. They were daring, they showed women's legs, and they infringed upon the morality-conscious Pageant officials.

Nevertheless, long before Bernie Wayne was inspired to pen those famous lyrics, "There she is, your ideal," judges at the Pageant were describing Miss America as "Ideal." Cole Phillips, an artist and illustrator who was a member of the Board of Judges, said that the selection of Miss Campbell "means the inauguration of a new type of American girl. Years ago there was the Gibson girl. The last few years the American ideal has been of two types, either the Flo Ziegfield type, or the Mary Pickford type. Neither of these . . . typify the American girl."

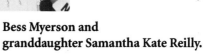

Bess Myerson and granddaughter Samantha Kate Reilly.

MARY CAMPBELL
MISS AMERICA 1922 AND 1923

Cole and his fellow artist judges (including Norman Rockwell) went on to describe the new ideal as "a rather tall girl with rather straight lines, fairly athletic, broad shoulders for swimming, a clear eye, and clear intelligent face. Measurements really mean nothing." Miss Campbell, five-feet-five-inches and weighing 120 pounds, apparently fit the bill. She was described as having "soft auburn tinted brown hair, well-chiseled features, white and pink complexion, and having size five gloves and size three shoes." Her proportions, according to judges, "approached perfection."

So there she was. The second Miss America. A sixteen-year-old high school student, chaperoned by her mother, who represented America's wholesome ideal. Little did organizers know how things would change within just a few short years.

Seizing on an old theatrical maxim — if you've got a good thing, run with it until the legs give out — Pageant organizers forged ahead with enthusiasm and a lot more money. In 1923, costs skyrocketed to $100,000 and the first grumblings about money erupted among Pageant organizers. Pageant official Samuel Leeds announced, "The committee will increase to twenty-five residents and not as in the past by a few directors who assumed financial responsibility by endorsing notes."

Mary Catherine Campbell made Pageant history that year by becoming the only contestant to win the title twice. The press announced "she successfully defended her laurels against seventy-four candidates, from hundreds selected in their own locality." Like her teenage predecessor, Margaret Gorman, Campbell eventually tired of the hoopla surrounding her victory and in a 1958 interview said, "I got so tired of the publicity, I didn't ever want to hear about Miss America again." As the event became larger and crowds thronged to the resort, festivities roared nonstop for a full three days.

Everything wasn't all fun and games. Pageant officials overlooked something so obvious they forgot to include it in the rules: "Miss America" was not supposed to be a "Mrs." She was, after all, touted as a "young maiden." That oversight prompted a rebellion when, according to the New York Times, "Several unnamed contestants made a formal demand for Miss Brooklyn's disqualification." Harry L. Godshall, director of the Pageant, ruled that Miss Brooklyn (Mrs. Everett Barnes) was eligible for the contest and free to hold the four prizes which she has won."

As things turned out, Mrs. Barnes wasn't the only married contestant. Miss Boston, Mildred Prendergast, showed up with her husband and infant, and Miss Alaska, Helmar Leiderman, was not only married, she was from New York City rather than Alaska! Pageant officials barred her from competition and were immediately slapped with a $150,000 lawsuit when Leiderman claimed "humiliating discrimination."

Rules were quickly amended, and to this day it's clear that "no one married,

Margaret Gorman returned in 1922 to defend her crown. Though she was a crowd favorite, she lost to Mary Catherine Campbell. Margaret, far right, is shown here with fellow hopefuls before the final competition in 1922.

or having been married, and no one having a child" is eligible for the competition.

Undeterred by such notoriety, the powers that be in Atlantic City recognized that the publicity surrounding the event was priceless, and they were not about to cave in. What started as a simple contest in a few local newspapers just kept on growing, and by 1924 spectators were treated to a five-day event which included eighty-three beauties who took part in a series of events, such as an American Beauty Ball, a Masked Night Carnival, and a Mardi Gras.

The original rolling chair parade now included floats to rival today's Rose Bowl parade, including a twenty-five foot, flower-adorned gondola and a huge replica of the GOP elephant in the center of a twenty-foot float (sponsored, of course, by the Republican Club). The most eye-stopping entry had to be the one sponsored by the Chamber of Commerce. It featured a giant papier-mâché male bather measuring eight feet at the waist sprawled out on a miniature beach. On top of him a girl in a swimsuit tickled his nose with a long stemmed rose. The sign on the side read "The Playground of the World Welcomes You."

BARBARA JO WALKER
MISS AMERICA 1947

Barbara and her husband, Dr. John Hummel, are the parents of two sons and one daughter and the grandparents of four grandchildren. Barbara still lives in her hometown, Germantown, Tennessee, where she works full-time as her husband's office manager.

I'm sure being Miss America has broadened my experience, but I have actually enjoyed being a past Miss America more than the year I reigned. Being on display was not my 'thing.' The most positive outcome has been my long association with a group of eight former Miss Americas. We get together for a long weekend as often as possible, and are a wonderful support group for each other. The biggest change in the Pageant is that the television extravaganza has come to rule the whole affair. It's lost its naturalness and spontaneity and today the contestants all seem to have been molded in the same form.

L–R: Barbara Jo Walker with daughter Sally and son Robert and husband Dr. John Hummel.

miss america speaks

And it did. It welcomed thousands and thousands of money-spending tourists, so that by 1925 contestants arrived in Atlantic City in a special train — nine Pullman cars carrying sixty-two contestants, who would strut their stuff for the next week in front of 300,000 people!

Flash bulbs popped and pictures flew across the country over the wires. Movie newsreels trumpeted the event in theaters across the country. It was inevitable that all the publicity would have a downside. With the Pageant's growing exposure came its inevitable detractors.

When Miss America 1924, Ruth Malcomson, refused to return the following year to defend her crown, claiming that "professionals" had edged their way into the all-amateur ranks of the Inter-City Beauties, she touched off a wave of accusations that sullied the reputation of the Pageant. These accusations, however, were not without merit; the magnitude of the event inevitably had attracted women who wanted to take home more than a golden mermaid and memories.

A Broadway showgirl named Kathryn Ray won the Miss Coney Island Pageant in which one of the judges was Earl Carroll, the producer of the show she was in. This drew cries of favoritism. More unfavorable speculation surfaced when professional actress Dorothy Knapp suddenly appeared in

Miss America 1925, Fay Lanphier (left), congratulates Miss America 1926, Norma Smallwood. Miss Smallwood and the two runners-up hold their beautiful two-foot silver urns that were part of the Pageant prizes for many years.

Left: Contestants and Pageant officials stroll the beach in Atlantic City in 1923.

Atlantic City to replace the original Miss Manhattan, who mysteriously dropped out of the competition.

Malcomson's refusal to defend her crown brought about still another change in Pageant rules. *The Atlantic City Daily Press* reported "The winner of this year's title will not be called upon next year to defend her crown, but will be invited to be a guest of honor together with previous Miss Americas."

While Pageant officials scurried about changing rules and procedures, they couldn't stop the onslaught of attacks hurled at its main attraction. It seemed every year brought more problems, and by the mid-twenties officials found themselves fending off attacks from religious groups and social groups, as well as grappling with increasing financial problems.

From its beginning, when spectators gasped at the sight of "young maidens" wearing "bathing costumes," the Pageant had always managed to confuse wholesomeness with sex appeal, creating a paradox that still exists.

Almost immediately following the first Pageant, women's social organizations cast a wary eye on the proceedings, declaring that "Modesty, which is

The maillot was braless and unstructured. It was usually made of wool — which clung to the body when wet — and was quite revealing. The beauties pictured were not Miss America contestants in 1923, but represented local theaters in one of the many events that were part of Pageant week.

BeBe Shopp
Miss America 1948

Married to Bayard Waring, Shopp lives in Massachusetts where she enjoys gardening, sewing, and painting. After winning the crown, she enjoyed a long career as a musician, lecturer, and television hostess. She is a licensed lay minister in the Episcopal Church, helps raise funds for the West Virginia Boys and Girls Club, and is a volunteer for VISTA. All four daughters, Kimberly, Laurie, Myalisa and Wendy, are married and together have produced eight grandchildren!

66

The Pageant changed my life for the best. It taught me confidence and organizational skills, and gave me the opportunity for my own television show. It's sometimes hard to always be Miss America, because people make certain assumptions about you before they get to know you. The Pageant has endured because of the vision of its founders and directors. It gives little girls a heroine who is a positive image — no small achievement in today's world!

99

one of the greatest safeguards of the Morals of the Nation, is being 'thrown to the winds' by the Miss America scoundrels."

With the crowning of the third Miss America, choir singer Ruth Malcomson, the YWCA protested that the rampant immodesty was going to be the ruin of "pure womanhood." By 1926, the Methodists had already written off the female participants as beyond saving, but feared that pictures of women in swimsuits would produce a "demoralizing effect on young men."

By the time 1927 rolled around, the Pageant had become a cause célèbre for women's and religious groups across the country. The Federation of Women's Clubs demanded an abandonment of the entire Pageant, pleading that "American women are sleeping while American girlhood is being degraded."

Bishop William J. Hafey of Raleigh, Maryland, speaking before the Atlantic City unit of the Catholic Daughters of America, called the Pageant "an exploitation of feminine charm by money-mad men," and demanded it be stopped. Other clergymen said the Pageant was "damaging to the morals of men, women, and children."

That same year, The Ocean City Camp Meeting Association adopted a resolution condemning the bathers' review. The resolution said, "The danger lies in taking girls of tender years and robing them in attire that transgresses the limit of morality." "The saddest feature of the affair," said Dr. Lake, head of the association, "is the willingness of a few businessmen to profiteer on the virtues of those of tender years . . . when men for the sake of a few pennies are willing to steal not only the brains, but the virtue and character of these tender years, it indeed becomes a tragedy."

The Atlantic City Federation of Church Women picked up the gauntlet and declared, "The beauty contest has an unwholesome moral effect on young women." The *New York Times* reported that the Federation sent a protest to the city commission and Pageant directors declaring, "In the interest of public welfare from both a moral and financial standpoint, we protest against the beauty pageant . . . we are persuaded that the moral effect on the young women entrants and the reaction generally is not a wholesome one."

Atlantic City had always been a magnet for summer visitors from Philadelphia, and that city's women were not about to risk exposing its male citizens to the scandalous sight of women parading in bathing costumes when they headed for the "shore" with wives and children in tow.

BeBe Shopp (top center) with husband Bayard Waring celebrating her mother's 90th birthday in 1993. Daughters Kimberly, Laurice, Myalisa and Wendy are with their husbands and their children.

miss america speaks

In March 1927, at a meeting attended by women leaders in educational, civic, religious, and social organizations, Philadelphia women sponsored a nationwide campaign to stop beauty pageants at Atlantic City. Proclaiming the demoralizing effect of the annual Pageant to be an established fact, the meeting deemed it "unworthy of a great resort like Atlantic City to adopt a method of advertising which involves the exploitation of young women."

When the General Federation of Women's Clubs in Los Angeles took similar action, the Pageant fired back. Frederick Hickman, president of the Chamber of Commerce said, "I regret to see that the Federation has criticized the Pageant . . . I am satisfied that this action was initiated by someone who has never seen the Pageant and was not familiar with the conditions under which the beauties compete and are entertained. Instead of having a demoralizing effect, the opposite is true, because it has been demonstrated to the young women of the country that the popular girl is the one who represents the highest ideals. The winner of the 1926 contest, Miss Norma Smallwood of Tulsa, Oklahoma, is a real combination of beauty, grace, and intelligence, artistic and refined. She is a type which the American girl might well emulate."

That answer, which has become the standard Pageant response to its critics to this day, didn't do much to appease its detractors. Things got worse. The Pageant became an embarrassment to the very hotel owners who had originally embraced the idea. They now deplored it as a scandalous, bawdy blight

How daring! In 1927, two members of Miss Atlantic City's court wore bobbed hair and only two were still wearing stockings! To prevent charges of favoritism, Miss Atlantic City was never a contestant, but was the official hostess for the event.

Ruth Malcomson, Miss America 1924 (holding bouquet) and Pageant officials. Armand T. Nichols (far right) was executive director of the Pageant from 1924 to 1933.

on their town. Julian Hillman, president of the Hotelmen's Association said, "There has been an epidemic recently of women who seek personal aggrandizement and publicity by participating in various stunts throughout the world, and the hotelmen feel that in recent years that type of woman has been attracted to the Pageant in ever-increasing numbers."

Atlantic City not only had to defend itself against charges of immorality; by 1928 there were complaints about the way Pageant financial affairs were conducted. Somebody had to pay for all those fireworks, flowers, special trains, carnivals, balls, and hotel accommodations, and the Pageant managed to find itself with a $52,000.00 deficit at the end of its first seven years.

Mayor Frederich Hechman and Harold Leves, representing the Pageant committee, made a valiant attempt to get support of the hotelmen's association for a 1929 Pageant. But, in a closed door meeting in 1928, the hotelmen voted not to continue to support the Pageant.

That was that. There she was — Miss America. And she wouldn't be heard from again for a very long time.

NORMA SMALLWOOD
MISS AMERICA 1926

Chapter Four

Turning Points

Is the Pageant a duck or a swan? I believe it's a swan, but too many people were beginning to perceive this as not just a duck, but an ugly duck that should have died a long time ago. Well, it almost died, but it didn't die, and we've always been able to pull it together and do what we had to do to make it a swan.

— LEONARD C. HORN
President and CEO
The Miss America Organization

Lenora

Lenora Slaughter—
the great transformer

In 1940, Frances Burke defeated thirty-eight contestants, who represented cities as well as states. It wasn't until 1959 that all fifty states selected a representative to compete in Atlantic City.

By 1927, it seemed throwing barbs at the Miss America Pageant was second only to baseball as America's national pastime. Whether it was because it was under fire, or because the criticisms were valid, the Pageant made a conscious attempt to clean up its act.

Sixty-nine contestants braved verbal and printed brickbats to make the trek to Atlantic City that year, and almost a third boasted some college affiliation. The winner that year, Lois Delander, Miss Illinois, was a sweet, seventeen-year-old high school honor student cut from the same mold as the first two teenage winners, Margaret Gorman and Mary Catherine Campbell.

After the Pageant, Delander picked up her scepter, four trophies, Bulova

THE GREAT TRANSFORMER

Lenora Slaughter, pageant director, welcomes 1955 contestants.

YOLANDE BETBEZE
MISS AMERICA 1951

Yolande Betbeze Fox lives in
Washington, D.C., and New York
City. She enjoyed a long career as an
opera singer, lecturer, and political
activist. Yolande is mother to a
daughter Yolande, and is enjoying
helping raise her baby grandchild,
also named Yolande.

*As an accomplished opera singer I
was one of the winners who helped
develop a serious image of Miss
America. Today the Pageant is run in
a more businesslike fashion and its
contestants and winners are treated
with much more respect. It's changed
in some ways — platform issue, less
emphasis on looks, more academic
focus — but basically it has lasted
because it essentially has stayed the
same. It's the integrity of the contestants, their simplicity and wholesomeness combined with drive and
ambition that make it as American as
apple pie.*

"

**Yolande Betbeze (r) with
daughter Yolande and granddaughter, also named Yolande.**

miss america speaks

**When the Pageant was revived in 1933, the country was in the throes of the Great
Depression, a time when people were looking for glamour and entertainment.
Marian Bergeron is shown here with her court of honor, judges, and radio
announcer Norman Brokenshire.**

watch, and Oldsmobile, and went home. She went on to college, got married,
and settled down — and that was that.

History buries its secrets, often deeply, and what isn't revealed is often
surmised. It seems possible, though no one will ever know, that even if a
public relations miracle convinced the public that the Pageant was as pure as
driven snow, the crowds still would not have flocked back to Atlantic City.

The country was in crisis. The stock market crash of 1929 was an event of
far greater magnitude than anything that was going on in Atlantic City. It sent
the country into a downward spiral, so it seems unlikely guests would have
filled the hotels or found the money to indulge in a week of festivities at the
shore. While grown men sold apples on the streets and the government
struggled to create jobs for millions, the Pageant slept, a dim memory in the
consciousness of a country with other things on its mind.

In 1933, a gallant attempt was made to revive the Pageant. Marian
Bergeron, the winner that year, looks back: "Sure there was no money around,
but everyone was tired of hearing about the hard times. Psychologically, it
came at a time when people were looking for glamour and entertainment."

Maybe. But things went wrong. The Hotelmen's Association refused to
support the Pageant, and without their backing, producing Miss America was
like trying to build a skyscraper without a foundation. Undaunted, Armand
Nichols, former secretary to the mayor, mustered the support of the mayor
and the City Council and took charge.

Anyone who thought the 1933 Pageant would wipe away the perception of chicanery or subterfuge was dreaming; it was a public relations nightmare. Thirty girls from twenty-eight states managed to make it to Atlantic City, but they arrived in a state of exhaustion. They were selected at local pageants held in amusement parks all over the country, and then sent on a seven-week vaudeville tour by the parks to recoup expenses.

The result was a Keystone Kops series of mishaps: Misses Maine and New Hampshire forgot their bathing suits; Miss Oklahoma had an attack of appendicitis and had to be rushed to the hospital; Miss New York State fainted from an infected tooth just as she was greeting the judges; Miss West Virginia suffered from a bad stomachache; Miss Arkansas was married; and Misses Iowa, Illinois, and Idaho were disqualified as nonresidents of the states they represented.

The presence of tabloid press reporters and other shady characters who hung around the sidelines clouded the event with an unseemly aura that helped doom the revival to failure. Bergeron, who was only fifteen at the time, recalls, "To make matters worse, the crown was stolen the night I won, and I never saw it again until it resurfaced in Atlantic City sometime around 1990."

The event was a financial disaster, but Bergeron, who had been singing on a New Haven radio station since she was twelve years old, went on to sing with Frankie Carle, Guy Lombardo, and Rudy Vallee, and even replaced Alice Faye for a while on CBS. She may have been one of the most talented Miss Americas, but when the Pageant was revived in 1935 it denied any association with the 1933 event, and refused to recognize Marian Bergeron as a true Miss America. "Actually, being just fifteen years old, I was a liability to the Pageant. I had nothing to give them. If I had been older I might have had some resentment, but at the time, I just didn't think all that much about it."

Today a grandmother of twelve granddaughters and one grandson, Bergeron says she has no regrets; she loves being part of the Miss America family and would do it all over again. Retired and living in Dayton, Ohio, Bergeron is still an outgoing and gregarious woman who devotes her time to volunteering with the hospice program and working with special children.

In the meantime, the people in Atlantic City had a staggering task ahead of them if they wanted to reinvent the pageant and crowd the boardwalk with the throngs of spectators present in the early twenties.

Showman Eddie Corcoran, promotional director for the Steel Pier, and his boss, Frank P. Gravatt, got the backing of three major figures to reorganize the event: hotelman John Hollinger, Chamber of Commerce President Louis Johnson, and City Commissioner William Casey. The Variety Club of Philadelphia agreed to conduct entry-level contests in other Variety Clubs and theaters across the nation.

The reorganized national Pageant, which would be staged on the Pier,

Crowned Miss America in 1927, Lois Delander looks every bit the demure seventeen-year-old high school honor student in her modest skirted bathing costume, complete with stockings and hat.

would be called "The Showmen's Variety Jubilee." But they needed something more than support from the community — they needed someone who could turn the pageant around, someone who could turn the duck into a swan. And they got her.

Lenora Slaughter, now retired and living in Arizona, recalls the mood of the times. "Women mostly didn't work outside the home then, but since I couldn't go to college, I had no choice, I had to go to work." Slaughter worked for the Chamber of Commerce in St. Petersburg, Florida. "We did everything we could to change the image of St. Petersburg as a place for old people only. Our local pageant was part of attracting tourists."

She did more than attract tourists; she attracted the attention of Eddie Corcoran who asked her to lend a hand in Atlantic City. She took a six-week leave of absence to head north, and she stayed until her retirement in 1967. The Miss America Pageant became her life's passion.

Elegant in a soft pink shirt and pearls, her white hair as beautifully coifed as that of any contestant, Lenora Slaughter Frapart reminisced about those days in a recent interview. "I wasn't thinking about the future potential of the Pageant. I saw what I didn't like, and I didn't have time to think about what I liked," she said. "First thing, I didn't like having nothing but swimsuits. I had to get Atlantic City to understand that it couldn't just be a beauty contest. I tried to make contestants realize it was an honor to be in the Pageant. That's what I wanted."

What she got was stinging notoriety when a sculptor unveiled a nude statue of that year's Miss America, Henrietta Leaver. Despite Leaver's emotional protest that she had posed for the statue in a bathing suit, the damage was done, and once again the Pageant had to fight for its reputation. Forty-nine years later a Miss America would be asked to forfeit her crown for posing in the nude, but in 1935 Leaver simply left Atlantic City and never returned — not even to pass on her crown to the new Miss America.

Lenora Slaughter was a fighter. She didn't waste time on the negatives; instead, she set out to build the Pageant on a solid foundation. Too many show business sharpies hanging around the festivities? No problem. She imposed regulations banning titles representing commercial interests such as newspapers, amusement parks, and theaters, and required contestants to compete under the title of a city, region, or state. Social organizations complaining about the young age of contestants? Slaughter fixed that: participation was limited to girls between the ages of eighteen and twenty-eight who had never been married. Parents reluctant to allow their daughters to be exposed to the nightlife of Atlantic City? Not to worry — Slaughter instituted a 1:00 A.M. curfew and banned all contestants from bars or nightclubs during Pageant week. And no Miss America would ever be seen smoking in public.

"She made all the right moves and put the Pageant on a respectable level,"

Bette Cooper as a contestant before winning the crown.

When eighteen-year-old Bette Cooper disappeared hours after she won the crown in 1937, photographers took this extraordinary official portrait the next morning — her robe and crown grace her throne, but no Miss America!

says Leonard Horn. "But no sooner than one crisis was solved, another would crop up." It's a miracle Lenora didn't just pack it in and head back to the relative calm of St. Petersburg after the Bette Cooper fiasco.

And what a fiasco that was! It began innocently enough. "We never had enough money," Slaughter recalls. "So we got some of the young men in town to help us out as chauffeurs." One of those young men, Lou Off, was the son of one of the city's movers and shakers and came with impeccable credentials. He was charmed by the young Miss Cooper and became her confidante as well as her chauffeur.

Cooper entered the Pageant on a lark and never expected to win. She was only eighteen, and about to enter her senior year at a private day school in the rural New Jersey community of Hackettstown. Cooper was stunned by her victory. She had no show business aspirations and was unwilling to forego a year of high school to fulfill her duties as Miss America.

Bette Cooper had won the crown, but she didn't want it, and she didn't know what to do about it. She only knew she had to get out of Atlantic City. Apparently her parents agreed, for they solicited Lou Off's help. Off and his friends secreted Cooper out of her hotel room in the middle of the night, and when photographers arrived to take a group photo of Miss America and her court the next morning they found an empty throne. While officials and

Lenora Slaughter helps Miss America 1959, Mary Ann Mobley, into her robe to the applause of fellow contestants.

police frantically searched for the missing queen, Cooper and Off watched the proceedings from a boat moored about two hundred feet off the Steel Pier.

By the time the dust settled, Bette Cooper was back home in Hackettstown and Slaughter had to face another challenge. Once again, she came up with an exquisite plan. The girls needed to be chaperoned in Atlantic City, and parents, although well-meaning, weren't always equipped to handle the job. Who then? Slaughter suggested that the most socially prominent women in town should organize and oversee a committee of chaperones. But "chaperone" recalled images of Spanish duennas, protecting convent schoolgirls from temptations of the flesh. That wasn't exactly, though also not far from, what Slaughter had in mind.

Many girls entered the Pageant with hopes of breaking into show business. They were ripe for unscrupulous "talent agents" and others who would exploit them. It was decided the term "hostess" had just the right amount of cachet. The mayor's wife, Mrs. C.D. White, agreed to head up a committee of the town's socialites provided she be granted complete control over contestants while they were in Atlantic City. Thus, the hostess committee, a mainstay of the Pageant to this day, was created. It was exactly what the Pageant needed to elevate the perceived moral character of the girls under its domain.

Slaughter also was responsible for adding talent to the competition, upgrading this portion of the total balloting, and moving the event into the Convention Center. "As long as we were on the Pier, we were just one more act that played the Pier," Slaughter says. "It took four years to make the move. The city was reluctant because we had to pay $10,000, but after Convention Hall saw what a benefit we were to them, they returned the money."

But Slaughter wasn't finished. At the time, local pageants were run by theaters, swimming pools, state fairs, amusement parks. She set out to change that. "I had to change the image. I did that by bringing in the local junior chamber of commerce — the Jaycees," she recalled. "Many parents wouldn't allow their daughters to compete. But we got the local Jaycees to talk to them, and once they understood what we were all about, we got less resistance."

Perhaps Slaughter's greatest legacy was introducing the college scholarship program. "We had the usual prizes — a Hollywood contract offer, maybe a fur coat, a chance to earn money modeling or working at the Pier. But not everyone wanted a Hollywood career. I wanted something that everyone could benefit from."

Jean Bartel, crowned Miss America in 1943, was a UCLA student who represented the kind of young woman the Pageant needed. "I was the first college girl to win the title," Jean Bartel says. "I was a member of the Kappa

Miss America 1949, Jacque Mercer, begins her year the morning after she is crowned. Lenora Slaughter, the other passenger in the official Miss America car, will be her almost constant companion.

Lenora Slaughter (below) in her office, flanked by Miss America portraits.

Lenora Slaughter greets parade
Grand Marshal Marilyn
Monroe in 1952.

Kappa Gamma Sorority, and we were invited to speak at a luncheon by sister sorority members at the University of Minnesota, and it was there that the idea of offering educational scholarships developed. Lenora Slaughter did a great job of returning with the idea and then selling it to the Board of Directors in Atlantic City."

Slaughter sat down and personally wrote about three hundred letters to big businesses asking for scholarship money. "I raised $5,000," she recalls. "It was hard, very hard to ask, but I couldn't go to college because of the Depression. It was my dream. I wanted it so bad for myself that I tried to see that every girl who wanted to go to college got the chance."

John Koushouris, the Pageant's television producer from 1962 to 1993, summed up Slaughter's contribution to the Pageant this way: "Lenora was an enigma. She ruled 'her girls' with an iron hand, exploited them when she had to, but was their fiercest defender. She could purr like a sweet Southern kitten, but if you crossed her, she could roar like a lion with a hangnail. She wasn't aware of her racial and social prejudices, but at the same time she was an effective crusader for the advancement of women. The girls trembled in her sight, but were in awe of her. She was a fierce businesswoman who could squeeze a nickel until the Indian cried, but she came to do a job, and by God, she did it."

She did it so well that when she retired in 1967 the state pageant directors panicked. The entire state organization was structured and devised by Slaughter. She was the one who enforced the feeling of family; she gathered in volunteers and looked after them like a mother hen. With her gone, the states organized themselves into the National Association of Miss America State Pageants to present a united front to the national board of directors in the event of any significant disputes or misunderstandings.

There was no need to worry. The national board of directors fostered the same degree of cooperation and sense of purpose that Slaughter began. The Miss America Organization could not exist without that vast army of volunteers serving the local and state pageants, and are steadfast in their commitment to support the states and to continue the relationship Lenora began.

The state and national offices share mutual goals, including a vision of the kind of young woman the states send to Atlantic City, the purpose and direction of the Pageant, and most of all, a trust between Pageant officials and the state and local organizations. That shared trust is an everlasting tribute to Lenora Slaughter.

JEAN BARTEL — MISS AMERICA 1943

The idea of offering educational scholarships was initiated at a Kappa Kappa Gamma Sorority luncheon in 1943, which Miss Bartel attended with Lenora Slaughter.

Bess

*Bess Myerson —
first Jewish
Miss America and
first scholarship
winner*

DECEMBER 7, 1941 . . . the day the world changed.

While much thought was given to discontinuing the Pageant for the
duration of the war, Board of Directors felt the event symbolized the spirit of
America and could be used to build morale.

Convention Center was taken over by the Air Force, a necessity of war, and
the Pageant moved to the Warner Theater. Chalfonte-Haddon Hall became
England General Hospital. All other hotels housed servicemen, and thousands of marching men replaced the glittering floats and bands that once
paraded on the boardwalk. Lights previously shining like a string of pearls
along the boardwalk were darkened, and lookout towers dotted the beaches
up and down the Jersey shore as Nazi submarines hovered off the coast.

BESS MYERSON — MISS AMERICA 1945

*Bess Myerson, the first scholarship winner, and her court (inset) pose in Catalina swimsuits
in front of the old Traymore Hotel.*

Bess Myerson sent her graduation picture for inclusion in the program book because she wanted to look different from all the other contestants. She succeeded and was crowned the new Miss America.

The Miss America Pageant became a symbol of hope to American soldiers. Miss America 1942, Jo-Carroll Dennison, was joined by twenty-nine fellow contestants in carrying this message of hope to every corner of the nation. They served their country in camps, hospitals, defense factories, USO Clubs, and Red Cross canteens.

Carmen D'Achino, a twenty-one year old from a small town in New Jersey, was away from home for the first time. "We were stationed down South," he says. "We were going to be shipped out in a few days, and we were all scared. We went to this show and I looked up and I saw this beautiful girl up there and I asked my friend who she was. And he said, 'that's Miss America,' and she made me want to cry because she reminded me of my girlfriend, and yet I was so happy she was there."

Jo-Carroll Dennison remembers the servicemen. "They came, they applauded, they smiled in a way that I had never experienced before," she said in a recent interview. "It was their country they were applauding. It was an awesome experience."

Jean Bartel, Miss America 1943, recalls, "I went on tour to fifty-three key cities and sold the most series E war bonds of anyone that year, and I received a special award from Secretary of the Treasury Morganthal. It was a proud time for Miss America."

A fierce hurricane slapped Atlantic City in 1944, causing massive destruction, but the resort pulled itself together to celebrate the end of the war the following year. That city always knew how to throw a party!

Lenora Slaughter's scholarship dream became a reality in 1945. Feminism enjoyed a brief awakening at that time. American manufacturers had not yet begun supplanting the manufacture of war machines with 'work saving' appliances that would lure American women away from careers and back into the kitchen.

Only 76,000 women graduated from colleges the year before the war ended. But women had spent the war years working at a variety of jobs, from building war machines and flying aircraft to serving in the armed forces and managing their own affairs, and after the war they began enrolling in college in record numbers. It was the perfect time for a pretty, talented, career-minded college graduate who needed money to continue her music studies, to be crowned Miss America. That woman was Bess Myerson.

Bess Myerson was not the typical Miss America contestant. She was both Jewish and from New York — not from some small hamlet in upper New York State, but from *New York City,* that hotbed of libertarianism and freethinking where the Bronx was up and the Battery down! All other contestants at the time came primarily from conservative families and grew up in small towns and rural areas. And they were Christian.

Myerson quickly assessed the situation. She knew she was the only girl in

the Pageant from a minority ethnic group. She felt uneasy in this WASP world, where the country club was closed to Jews and neighborhoods were carefully guarded against encroachment by Jewish people.

Myerson remembers: "I lived in a housing complex in the Bronx where everyone was Jewish, and almost everyone's parents spoke with an accent. My mother wouldn't even go to Atlantic City where she would have to eat unfamiliar food, and then I walk into this room and here were these girls with real 'American' parents, doting all over them. And while I carried my things to Atlantic City in shopping bags, the other girls had matched luggage. Then there were the hostesses with their white gloves and hats and their upper-crusts accents. It was a world I knew nothing about, and I sensed they knew nothing about me and my world."

"I was aware of anti-Semitism, but had never been a target of it myself, so it wasn't a big issue with me at the time. Then Jews who gathered at my hotel were talking about the Holocaust and about caricatures of Jews with long noses and ugly faces and they said 'please show them a Jew can be beautiful.' And when Al Gold, the official Atlantic City photographer said, 'Bessie you have to hang in there. Nobody down here wants you to win, but I want to photograph a Jewish Miss America,' I knew I was just as much a target as any Jew anywhere."

During the war, Convention Center became a military training center and the Pageant moved to the Warner Theater on the Boardwalk. Bess Myerson, soon to be crowned Miss America, is fourth from left in the swimsuit competition.

Crowned Miss America at the end of the war, Bess Myerson went on the road to sell Victory Bonds.

Eveyln Ay
Miss America 1954

Married forty years on November 13, 1994, to Carl G. Sempier, she is the mother of two daughters, Carlyn Ay Darby and Stacy Leigh. Today Eveyln Ay is homemaker, wife, mother, grandmother, lecturer, charity fund raiser, gardener, community activist, nursing home board member, and active churchgoer.

The impact on my life from having been Miss America sets me apart; it's been positive and rewarding. One difficulty is being prejudged by people as Miss America instead of being judged for being me! I believe the Pageant has endured because its scholarship program makes it worthwhile, the thousand of volunteers across the country give it credence, and the Pageant has not strayed from its original concept of recognizing outstanding women of character, intellect and beauty. In my era, women had limited career opportunities and were expected to marry and raise families. Today women have choices, and the Pageant has reflected and encouraged those choices.

99

L–R: Carlyn Sempier Darby, Carl G. Sempier, Evelyn Ay, Stacy Leigh Sempier.

miss america speaks

Bess Myerson wowed the judges with her rendition of Grieg's Piano Concerto in A minor during the talent competition.

When Lenora Slaughter came to New York to watch a rehearsal for the Miss New York City Pageant, she suggested Bess change her name. Myerson remembers the incident: "I was startled. The thought had never occurred to me. A lot of show business people changed their names at that time, so I never knew exactly what Lenora's motives were, but I wondered if she had ever made the same suggestion to any other contestant. Somehow I knew suddenly that I wasn't dealing with just a name change. The Pageant wanted someone for their first scholarship award that had an acceptable talent, and I was already playing in concerts at the time. They wanted a winner, and if they thought my being Jewish was a detriment, then changing my name would have been one way not to have to deal with the issue. My decision not to change my name was instinctive. I thought, 'I can't give up my roots, because I'm going to get tangled in them.' I was a Jew and proud of it and I was going to stay a Jew. I was already losing my sense of who I was; already I was in a masquerade, marching across stages in bathing suits. I kept telling myself it was okay, that if that's what I had to do to win, then I could do it. But whatever was left of myself I had to keep; I sensed that I had to keep my name."

Myerson didn't know at the time how much keeping her name meant to the Jewish community in this country. It became even more of an issue after World War II. In 1945 Americans learned that something monstrous had happened during the war: ovens . . . gas chambers . . . mass graves. And the numbers! Millions of Jews, along with gypsies, the disabled, nuns, priests, rabbis, homosexuals, and political opponents.

American Jews ached for good news, for something that would give them hope. And when the Jewish community heard there was a Jewish contestant in the Miss America Pageant, many came to Atlantic City to see for her for themselves. When Myerson won, the audience went wild and cries of "Mazel tov" rang out in the theater.

Vicki Gold Levi, daughter of photographer Al Gold, was five years old the night Bess won. Vicki recalls: "I remember being a little bewildered by the whole thing, but my father said, 'Be proud little girl, Miss America is Jewish, like us.' All those years taking pictures of Miss America — and finally — finally — a Jewish Miss America. It meant so much to him. To all of us."

And so the twenty-one-year old girl from the Bronx, who wowed the crowd with her rendition of "Summertime" on the flute and Grieg's Piano Concerto in A Minor on the piano in the talent competition, became the first college graduate to be a Miss America, the first scholarship winner, and the first Jewish Miss America.

And what a fabulous Miss America she was! For twelve years, she hosted the Miss America Pageant. She also hosted a national television show, appeared on popular television programs of the 1960s, has been widely published, and held a number of public offices in New York City.

Above: Official Atlantic City photographer Al Gold urged Bess Myerson to stay in the competition. A favorite of all the winners he photographed, he strikes a playful pose with BeBe Shopp, Miss America 1948.

Top: Five-year-old Vicki Gold was Bess Myerson's page when she returned to crown the new Miss America in 1946, the year the Pageant returned to Convention Center.

Vanessa

*Vanessa Williams—
changing the face
of America*

SEGREGATION. That word conjures up images of separate schools, separate drinking fountains, separate units in the Armed Forces, separate seating on buses, separate churches. And in the world of competitions, separate pageants.

Bess Myerson was right to feel uneasy at finding herself in a WASP world the day she arrived in Atlantic City, an area settled by Quakers — some of whom still owned some of its finest hotels. The Pageant struggled in the twenties and thirties to rid itself of its early tawdry image. One of the ways it chose to counteract that image was to focus on family credentials as proof of the wholesomeness of its contestants. As late as 1945, when Myerson competed,

VANESSA WILLIAMS—MISS AMERICA 1984

Debra Maffett, Miss America 1983, crowns Vanessa Williams, the first African American Miss America.
Vanessa's First Runner-Up, Suzette Charles, was also African American.

all contestants were required to list, on their formal biological data sheet, how far back they could trace their ancestry.

No wonder Myerson felt uneasy! While some past contestants could claim a lineage going back to the Revolutionary War — and one claimed ancestry right back to the Mayflower — there she was, a first generation American, daughter of Russian/Jewish immigrants, chaperoned by one of Atlantic City's elite hostesses, competing with Southern belles, and New England blue bloods.

Of course, for native born Americans whose ancestry predated that of any daughter of the Revolution, it was another story altogether. Glenn Osser, musical director of the Pageant from 1955 to 1987, recalls: "Before my time — probably as far back as 1926 — the Pageant had an American Indian Queen, called 'Princess America.' She didn't compete, she was just part the entertainment. Around 1957 we wrote some solo numbers for her as a divertissement, and she was called, 'Miss Indian America.' But she never was a contestant."

In 1941, a Native American, Mifaunwy Shunatona, represented Oklahoma at the Pageant, and even won the "Miss Congeniality" title. However, there would not be another Native American contestant for almost thirty years.

No matter how uncomfortable Myerson might have felt, at least she was eligible to compete. This wasn't an option for young black American women. If you were black, forget it. It wasn't as subtle as the anti-Semitism Myerson sensed; it was right there in the rule book. Rule seven: "Contestants must be of good health and of the white race."

Kimberly Aiken, Miss America 1994, reflected on that time. "My grandparents always watched the Miss America Pageant, but they never dreamed that one day their own granddaughter would be Miss America. It was an impossible dream back then," she says. Lencola Sullivan, Miss Arkansas 1980, and the first African American to make the top five echoed that sentiment, "I grew up watching the Miss America Pageant faithfully every year, and I never saw anyone who looked like me, even though beauty does come in all different colors, shades, and ethnic backgrounds."

If you look closely at early photographs, you will see there were African Americans in the Pageant — black men served as "slaves" in the Court of Neptune, pushing the chairs on the boardwalk, and playing the banjo or horn on early floats in the parade.

Shut out of the Pageant by racism and bigotry, and awakened by a new sense of self which was fostered by the civil rights movement of the sixties, blacks set up their own contest in 1968. In an article in the *New York Times,* September 1968, J. Morris Anderson, an organizer of the black pageant said, "There's a need for the beauty of the black woman to be paraded and applauded as a symbol of universal pride." Saundra Williams, an eighteen-year-old sociology major and winner of the Miss Black America Pageant says, "Miss America does not represent us because there has never been a black girl

When Vanessa Williams won, it caused a whole group of people to dare to dream. People who had not dared dream before for fear of being disappointed.

— DEBBYE TURNER
MISS AMERICA 1990

Black "slaves" appeared with Miss America and King Neptune in 1921.

in the Pageant. With my title, I can show black women that they, too, are beautiful. We keep saying that over and over because for so long none of us believed it, but now we're finally coming around."

Lenora Slaughter recalls, "When they started their own pageant I gave them help and advice and I complimented them." What Slaughter failed to recognize at the time was that African Americans were not looking for compliments; they were looking for acceptance. "We're protesting because the beauty of the black woman has been ignored; it hasn't been respected," Anderson explained in the aforementioned article. Looking back, Slaughter remembers it differently. "When we opened up the Pageant to blacks, I learned there were many beautiful black girls and they are equal." Of course, that was something people of color knew all along.

Lest we judge Pageant officials too harshly, we must remember this was another era. It was a time when, if you were Jewish or black or Italian, you weren't likely to get into medical school, or have your wedding announcement accepted in the *New York Times*. A time when Japanese Americans living on the West Coast were torn from their homes and sent to internment camps. A time when education was separate and unequal.

America was a society built on elitism and money, and the Pageant was as much a prisoner of its times as a leader. The idea was to produce a Miss America who could sell. And what America was selling was a postcard picture of white America.

Yolande Betbeze, Miss America 1951, recalls, "It was unheard of in the fifties to have blacks in the Pageant and I was very vocal about that. I marched for civil rights, and took part in sit-ins in Woolworth's in New York. Pageant officials weren't very happy about it, but I had to speak out, and eventually change came."

Change didn't come easily in America, or to the Miss America Pageant, but long before 1984, when the first African American won the crown, women like Irma Nydia Vasquez, Yun Tau Zane, Keungsuk Kim, and Susan Supernaw were breaking racial barriers. Vasquez was Miss Puerto Rico in 1948, Zane was the first Asian contestant, representing Miss Hawaii that same year, and Kim was the first Korean American to make the top ten finalists, representing Wisconsin in 1981.

In an article in *The Press of Atlantic City*, September 1994, Supernaw, who was Miss Oklahoma 1971, said her family was "dirt poor" and she didn't know what the Pageant was or how to become a part of it. "I didn't know how to walk in high heels because I never wore them. I borrowed a dress and used my gymnastic skills for my talent." Supernaw didn't win the crown that year

Top: Miss Princess America didn't compete; she was part of the entertainment as far back as 1926 when Norma Smallwood won the crown.

Above: Miss Princess America, circa late 1950s.

YOLANDE BETBEZE
MISS AMERICA 1951

DEBBYE TURNER
MISS AMERICA 1990

MARJORIE VINCENT
MISS AMERICA 1991

CHERYL BROWNE
MISS IOWA 1970

and she didn't make it into the ten semifinalists. She and an African American contestant each won a $1,500 award, and to this day she wonders if the award was created to fend off charges of racism. "We never got a straight answer about what the judge's award was for," Supernaw says. "In our minds it meant, 'Don't think we are prejudiced, but we are.'"

Cheryl Browne, Miss Iowa 1970, the first African American to win a state title and make it to Atlantic City opened the doors for her sisters. Miss Delaware 1976, Deborah Lipford, was the first African American to make the top ten, and Lencola Sullivan, Miss Arkansas 1980, was the first African American to make the top five.

But it was Vanessa Williams, a beautiful, gifted, and unknown twenty-year-old from Millwood, New York, who broke the final barrier in 1983 to become America's first black Miss America. In one of those strange coincidences which no one can predict or explain, after so many years of being shut out of the Pageant, two black women represented Miss America that year. Vanessa's First Runner-Up, Suzette Charles, a native of Mays Landing, New Jersey, reigned the last eight weeks of that year after Williams resigned the crown.

YUN TAU ZANE
MISS HAWAII 1948

IRMA NYDIA VASQUEZ
MISS PUERTO RICO 1948

DEBORAH LIPFORD
MISS DELAWARE 1976

Suzette Charles, First Runner-Up to Vanessa Williams, became Miss America during the last eight weeks of Vanessa's year.

Left: Miss Arkansas, Lencola Sullivan, Miss Oklahoma, Susan Powell, and Miss Washington, Doris Janell Hayes display their trophies after the final night of preliminary competition. Miss Arkansas, the first African American to make top five, won the swimsuit competition, and Miss Oklahoma and Miss Washington tied for first place in the talent competition. Miss Oklahoma, Susan Powell, went on to become Miss America 1981.

The third African American woman to wear the crown was Debbye Turner, Miss America 1990, who competed for nearly eight years through eleven tries in two states to finally make it to the national Pageant. She was followed by Marjorie Vincent, who was not only black, but the daughter of Haitian immigrants.

Kimberly Aiken broke another barrier when the crown was placed on her head: she was the first African American contestant from a former confederate state to become Miss America. She won her hometown pageant in 1993, then went on to win the Miss South Carolina contest in July 1993.

Virginia Cha, Miss Maryland 1989, the first Asian American to be First Runner-Up at the national competition says, "Twenty or thirty years ago it wasn't possible to have women of all races and ethnic backgrounds in the Pageant, but now that we do we shouldn't be surprised that the Pageant is in step with the rest of the world. For an example, in 1994 a hearing-impaired woman became Miss America. Why should that be such a surprise? A hearing-impaired contestant made top ten my year . . . so it was just a matter of time. It just simply should not be an issue now; we should move on and not lose sight of the Pageant's goal."

Karen Aarons sums it up this way: "Diversity comes out of the local competitions. They represent the mores of their communities, so the change comes from the bottom up. You have to wait for local communities to catch up with the changes in the nation, and as the nation changes, we change."

Television

Enter television

So there it was ... every September, the first Saturday after Labor Day, almost 15,000 people filled Convention Center to cheer their favorites and watch the stage show of the Miss America Pageant in Atlantic City. It was no ordinary event; it was both entertainment and a social gathering where people gathered to witness the spectacular culmination of many months of work.

It was work that combined the resources of the area's socialites, who volunteered their time to serve as hostesses, the stage producers and directors, and all those local and state pageant volunteers across the country. Together, they put on a hell of a show, and everyone was happy.

Moviegoers could see the highlights of the crowning of the new Miss America in movie newsreels, and the Sunday newspapers always ran a picture

B E F O R E   T E L E V I S I O N

*Before there was television, there was radio. Here Norman Brokenshire broadcasts from
the steps of Atlantic City High School in 1927.*

LEE MERIWETHER
MISS AMERICA 1955

Lee Meriwether and her husband
Marshall Borden live in California.
Her daughter, Kyle Oldham, is the
proud mother of Ryan Isabelle
Oldham, born in 1993. Another
daughter, Lesley Aletter, is an art
student. Lee began her show business
career immediately after winning
the Miss America title and has
appeared in numerous television
and stage shows and films. She has
served as Honorary Chairman of
the Crippled Children's Society, and
National Education Chairman of the
American Cancer Society and the
Cystic Fibrosis Foundation.

"

*The Pageant gave me confidence that
anything was possible, even for a
young girl like me who had always
thought of herself as plain, skinny,
and awkward. The money I earned
enabled me to study acting, and the
opportunities I had to represent
sponsors led directly to my television
and film career. My only regret is that
I didn't keep a journal with the names
of all the wonderful people I met along
the way. It isn't only Miss America who
benefits, but as the pageant matured,
it has given thousands of young women
a springboard to unlimited options
for their education and future. Today
every state representative has a golden
opportunity to 'make a difference.'*

"

miss america speaks

and story the day after the Pageant. So for that one moment, before the main movie started, before readers turned the page, Miss America shone in the public eye. This brief exposure would change. Broadcast media was expanding. Television exploded on the scene. An industry was launched; a nation, and the Miss America Pageant, were transformed.

Television news was bringing a new immediacy to world events, and it was bringing it right into America's homes. The little box that moviemakers scorned and intellectuals ignored was slowly but surely encroaching upon American lives and psyches. In 1954 there were an estimated 1,000 television sets per every 26,000 homes. Atlantic City could no longer resist television's appeal.

At that time the ABC television network was in its infancy and was in competition with the giants of television, NBC and CBS. ABC needed a crowd-pleaser, and the Pageant needed a network. Timing, sometimes, is everything.

ABC had previously attempted to secure the rights to televise the national finals for five thousand dollars, but Pageant officials were afraid they would lose revenue from their large live audience if people could stay home and watch it for free.

A chance meeting between Pageant president Hugh Wathen and the renowned band leader Paul Whiteman in a Penn-Atlantic Hotel lounge turned the tide. Whiteman was an entertainment consultant for the American Broadcasting Company and he discussed the possibility of an ABC broadcast with Wathen. The problem was financing. Both men realized a corporate sponsor would be necessary, and Whiteman pitched the idea to the president of the Philco company the very next day. He was able to convince that corporation of the Pageant's appeal to the television viewer — those millions of unseen people across the land who were not only viewers — but consumers. And what they were looking at and buying was television sets. Philco purchased the rights to the show for $10,000, and then contracted to have ABC broadcast the event. Not missing an advertising beat, Philco promoted its sponsorship with a new line of Philco "Miss America" television sets.

1954 was a year of American innocence. The memories of war had faded. Eisenhower was president. America was looking forward to peace and prosperity. It was a time of optimism. And so it came to be that in that year, on the American Broadcasting Company, Lee Ann Meriwether, was crowned Miss America 1955, the first ever to be crowned on live television. The Pageant was changed forever.

Changes were gradual rather than immediate, inching along, with slow, grudging concessions to the demands of increasing television technology. Marks clearly needed someone with expertise in live television, and Alexander Cantwell, then vice president in charge of live production at BBDO advertising in New York, was hired to produce the stage show.

L–R: Daughter Kyle Oldham holding Ryan
Isabelle, husband Marshall Borden, Lee
Meriwether, daughter Lesley Aletter.

Eddie Fisher (far right) was a guest at the 1953 Pageant.

For five weeks of the year, Cantwell took up residence in Atlantic City and created the Pageant's stage show: a live theatrical event that also met the requirements of television.

The cameras filmed the event in black and white. They were primitive by today's standards. Four or five cameras set up on tripods around the stage in a way that would cause the least amount of disruption to the live audience's view of the show.

The Pageant staff firmly held to Marks' edict that television was only a guest — the stage show was the first consideration. Therefore, the television staff's only opportunity to come on stage was on Saturday morning after the Pageant's three preliminary shows were completed.

Despite primitive equipment and technical restraints, the Miss America Pageant was capturing the hearts and ratings of the television audience. In 1957, the Pageant moved to CBS, and the following year CBS expanded the show from ninety minutes to two hours. In 1962, Cantwell hired John Koushouris, a pioneer in television technology, to co-produce the Pageant with the CBS producer, Paul Levitan.

Looking back, Koushouris reminisces: "How we ever got a ninety-minute live show on the air with only one day's camera rehearsal was a miracle. The schedule was harrowing." Koushouris continued to work with Levitan until

1964, when he became the sole television producer for the Pageant and CBS.
Cantwell continued to produce the stage show.

Koushouris explains that the Pageant had the stage for rehearsals and for
preliminary night competitions which were held on Wednesday, Thursday,
and Friday nights. On Friday night the television crew came in and made the
necessary changes to accommodate the cameras. Then the equipment would
be hand carried from a truck onto an area to the left side of the stage.

A black curtain hung from the ceiling creating a room about thirty feet by
thirty feet in which the portable camera equipment, audio facilities, and
control panel were set up on folding tables. Another folding table was set up
for the production staff. Everything ran out of six black and white cameras.
The cameras all sat on pedestals, as no cranes or other sophisticated equipment were available.

"We had camera facilities from early Saturday morning to a couple of
hours before air and that was it. I was constantly reminded that the Pageant
was a stage show, and television its guest, but if that was true it was the guest
who came to dinner, and not only stayed, but ate everything in sight,"
Koushouris says.

With the advent of color in 1966, the telecast moved to NBC and the hand-
carried equipment was eliminated, replaced by technical equipment housed
in a huge mobile truck. The television picture was still transmitted to New
York by land lines over telephone wires. This method of transmission was
replaced by satellite in the mid-eighties.

1966 brought additional changes. Cantwell left the show and George
Cavalier, who was the California Pageant stage producer, was brought to
Atlantic City to take his place.

"Initially it worked out very well," Koushouris says. "We did wonderful
shows — we did book shows in those years, and we did theme shows. But
television was becoming more intrusive. No matter how hard the Pageant
tried to ignore it, it would not go away."

In 1964, Koushouris developed a very small camera which was positioned
on a lighting grid forty feet high and was run by remote control. "It was one of
the first overhead shots in television," Koushouris says. It was almost a decade
later before he was able to bring in a small crab crane for the center runway
which would allow for camera shots from a height of eight or nine feet. About
the same time, he was able to persuade the Pageant organizers to allow
another remote camera on a long pole at the end of the runway to give the
viewing audience a panoramic shot of Convention Center. Resistance to this
latter development came from a fear of obstructing the live audiences' view of
the stage. Koushouris prevailed, and eventually was allowed to move his
cameras around the stage for greater, more flexible coverage.

Koushouris further explains, "At the beginning we had no effects equipment

Debra Barnes poses for the television camera in 1967 while newspaper photographers and radio announcers vie for her attention.

as we now know it. We had mechanical faders and that was it. The lighting has come full circle from huge lights that were mounted on one rail and generated a lot of heat, to the small units that are today controlled by computers. Now there are rails going out over the runway, up the stage, down stage, and all of these lights are automated."

Koushouris pushed for wireless microphones, almost unheard of at the time, and was among the first to use electronically controlled zoom lenses. Today preprogrammed computers control both lighting and video special effects. The televised Pageant has enjoyed the evolution of technology, from the early tripods of the fifties to the steadi-cam which revolutionized live camera shooting in the nineties.

From its inception until 1989, the Pageant's music was performed live; for much of that time, from 1955 until 1986, this live musical performance fell under the direction of Glenn Osser. "He was an absolute genius," Koushouris says, "and his wife, Edna Osser, was a brilliant lyricist. She would be the one

MARILYN VAN DERBUR
MISS AMERICA 1958

Marilyn and her husband, attorney Lawrence Atler, live in Denver, Colorado. Their daughter, Jennifer, attends Georgetown Law School in Washington. After winning the crown, Marilyn returned to the University of Colorado where she graduated with Phi Beta Kappa honors. For twenty-five years Marilyn has been in great demand as a keynote convention speaker, and for sixteen years she was the only woman guest lecturer for General Motors.

Marilyn is the co-founder of the American Coalition for Abuse Awareness, a grassroots national organization based in Washington, D.C., that is dedicated to strengthening the laws protecting adult survivors and child victims of sexual abuse. In addition, in 1993, Marilyn co-founded ONE VOICE, a nonprofit organization also based in Washington, D.C., where survivors, therapists, and child advocates are joined together nationally to speak with one voice to end the sexual violations of children through public education and awareness.

66

Being named Miss America over three decades ago still gives me access to network television shows, newspapers, and national medical and judicial conferences. In 1991 when the story leaked that I was an incest survivor, I thought my life was over. Now there is no doubt in my mind that I am part of a bigger plan ... that I was named Miss America so long ago to enable me to do the work I am now doing. When children cry out to me that if this could happen to Miss America, maybe they aren't so ugly and bad, then I know that the title transcends any possible negative. I believe the show has endured because young women prepare for it as if their future depends on it — and many times it does!

99

Marilyn Van Derbur (r) with daughter Jennifer and husband Lawrence Atler.

miss america speaks

who came up with the basic concept of the shows in those years, and working with George Cavalier, the script and music and staging would be built around her concepts."

Osser, who began working with the Pageant in 1955, says, "We didn't have production numbers at first. Bert did some solo numbers, but there was no dancing. We did have name guests — Eddie Fisher was the guest my first year."

It wasn't until 1960 that the head of the Alabama Pageant conceived a production number performed to an original score. Bernie Wayne began writing songs, which were sung by Bert Parks and former Miss Americas. This continued until George Cavalier came aboard in 1966 and began doing "book" shows. In 1968, Edna Osser joined the program and began writing original lyrics. The concept of including production numbers in the show took hold.

Convention Center may be a great place for hockey games, but it's probably the worst place in the world for television acoustics. Consequently, Cantwell deigned that the music for the production numbers be prerecorded. Several weeks before the show Osser would assemble an orchestra and would prerecord the music for all of the production numbers in New York, though a live orchestra was still used both for the talent numbers and to play in and out of station breaks during the telecast.

When NBC began televising the event, they supplied everything needed for the telecast: mobile units, technicians, sets, lights, and audio facilities. Koushouris even had an office at NBC for himself and two of his assistants.

Koushouris looks back: "It was a fairy tale marriage until NBC started cutting back. Ratings were beginning to slip, the show did not sell as easily as it had in the past." So a new system was initiated. Koushouris suggested to Marks that the Pageant be the sole television producer and supply the show to NBC as a completed package. The Pageant would sell the time on NBC to sponsors and then, in turn, buy the time on NBC in which to place its show. John Koushouris' production company would become the production arm of the Pageant and would independently supply all television facilities.

Time and familiarity eroded resistance, and the Pageant staff began making more and more concessions to television. "I convinced Marks that we should present the preliminary shows on Tuesday, Wednesday, and Thursday, thereby giving us all day Friday and Saturday to rehearse cameras on-stage," Koushouris says. "We went from taking Polaroid pictures of the contestants during their talent rehearsals to taping all of the talent numbers during preliminary nights to give the director a better idea of how to stage the eventual ten semi-finalists who would present their talent on television the night of the air show."

Even with the enormous acceptance by television viewers, Marks was adamant about pre-taping any portion of the show. Koushouris says, "I worked with the inventors of television tape at CBS and I wanted to use tape as a tool to better tell the Miss America Story." But Al Marks laid down the law. "Do not leave the live stage, ever" was his edict. Koushouris persisted. "After a few years I showed Al Marks some combined pictures with Miss America live, and in the upper right hand corner Miss America on tape showing the viewing audience what she did during the year of her reign. So he said, 'Okay, but don't ever leave the live stage.'"

There were several months of preparation before the production team arrived in Atlantic City. Crews had to be hired, contracts drawn, sets designed, scripts written, music and commercial announcements recorded, opening graphics designed and executed, and the technical foundation laid in Convention Center. However, until the end of 1992, the television production staff arrived in Atlantic City only nine days before air time. During those short nine days, the staff coordinated all their efforts and produced a two-hour live television show.

"I put together a top team — Tim Kiley, director; Charles Lisanby, designer; Don Pippin, musical director; Scott Salmon choreographer; Angela Osborne, coordinating producer; John Calabrese, field producer; and a great technical crew. That's what made it all possible," Koushouris says. He was able to take a huge space and crank it into a studio that transferred it from an enormous, dark, cavernous structure into the television fairyland viewers saw and loved.

Marks once modestly suggested that his involvement in the marriage of Miss America and television began "more by accident than design. I wore the hat of executive producer for stage and television," says Marks, "because then you could have absolute control — veto power if you will. I suppose you could call it a benevolent dictatorship."

That dictatorship, with the increased television responsibilities, was exhausting. Up until then, Marks, an Atlantic City stockbroker, worked as an unpaid volunteer and began looking for a replacement so he could retire.

LEE MERIWETHER
MISS AMERICA 1955

Miss America 1956, Sharon Kay Ritchie (third from left) and other contestants smile for the camera.

Don't ever forget that television is a guest on our stage. This is a news event and you are here to televise it as such, but our Pageant is and will always be a live theatrical event.

— ALBERT A. MARKS JR.
*Chairman and CEO
The Miss America
Organization 1967–1987*

Don Pippin, music director 1979–199

Top: Albert A. Marks Jr., left, the late chairman and CEO (1967–1987) of the Miss America Organization, with John L. Koushouris.

Above: The late George Cavalier, field director and stage show producer from 1961–1986, with John Koushouris.

Right: Glenn (Abe) Osser and orchestra in 1960.

Above: Choreographer Anita Mann directs contestants during rehearsal of the swimsuit production number.

Right: Rehearsing the television show in 1992. Top row: Choreographer Scott Salmon, television director Tim Kiley, assistant Ames Christopher, national production manager Bill Caligari. Bottom: field producer John Calabrese.

Top: Virginia Cha, Miss Maryland 1989, rehearsing with choreographer Scott Salmon.

Above: Tim Kiley, television director 1979–1992.

Top: Stage manager Peter Margolis cues the opening production number during the 1994 telecast.

Above: Tish Byrnes eliminates possible mayhem, organizing some of the many gowns and costume changes backstage.

John L. Koushouris

Associate director Christine Clark and director Jeff Margolis in 1994.

When NBC began televising the event in 1966, hand-carried equipment was replaced by technical equipment housed in a huge mobile truck, pictured here in 1986. Today modern satellite equipment transmits the telecast.

MARY ANN MOBLEY
MISS AMERICA 1959

Mary Ann and husband Gary Collins celebrated their 28th wedding anniversary in 1994. Daughter Clancy, a Stanford graduate, is an executive in the movie industry. Mary Ann is a working actress who has performed on stage, in film, and on television. She was appointed to the National Council on Disability by President Bush, and has been on the board of the National March of Dimes for thirty years. She is a member of the board for the National Crohn's and Colitis Foundation and the Susan G. Komen Breast Cancer Foundation, and she wrote and produced a documentary for World Vision, an international relief organization. She is most proud of the Mary Ann Mobley Pediatric Wing at the Rankin General Hospital in her hometown.

66

Everything about being Miss America has been positive. I came from a small town in Mississippi and then I had this great opportunity to see all of America and even to travel overseas. I worked as much after my year as I did during my year because the title opened a lot of doors for me. I think the greatest change is a lack of the spontaneity and fun that we used to have up there on that stage. Bert Parks really interacted with us, and knew how to get a laugh from any situation. Today, the contestants seem so well versed in their platforms that there are no surprises. The Pageant will continue to last as long as the local and state pageant volunteers have the will to devote all the time and energy it takes to send great contestants to Atlantic City.

99

miss america speaks

In 1987, Leonard C. Horn replaced Al Marks. Koushouris, praising Marks for ushering in the Pageant through the difficult years and making it a highly rated television show, also recognizes Horn as the one who "brought the Pageant from the Victorian age into the 20th century, giving television and its technology an opportunity to create a show that could compete with the most sophisticated presentation on television."

According to Jeff Margolis, the Pageant's television producer since 1993, the Miss America Pageant is unique in television among large special events. While most require ten or twelve weeks of full-time preparation, Pageant employees begin work eleven months before air. What happens in Atlantic City on the televised show affects what goes on throughout the year at the state pageants.

"By Christmas following the September show we have to have the concept and rundown completed for the next year's show so that the Pageant can let all the states know how the show will change," Margolis explains. "Once Mr. Horn approves the concept and rundown, we're off and running. Our initial production staff is about fifteen people, but by the time we move to Atlantic City, the stage crew, technical crew, production staff, stage managers, director, two assistant directors, and various support staff total about 150 people. A video truck contains state-of-the-art video, camera, tape, and switching facilities. "We hire all technical, audio, camera people, and stage crews directly, because people who know they are hand picked will give the most to the show," Margolis explains.

Although some of the stage technicians arrive in Atlantic City several weeks ahead to begin preparations, the production staff and the contestants arrive in Atlantic City only thirteen days before air. The contestants immediately begin rehearsal with the choreographer in a separate rehearsal space, and Margolis sees them on stage in Convention Center exactly one week before show time.

"We start blocking the show in the rehearsal hall without cameras, then we block all day Thursday, Friday and Saturday morning. On Saturday afternoon we have a complete dress rehearsal," he explains.

All pre-taping is done in California and Philadelphia, with Marks' restriction that all taped segments be inserted into a live picture no longer in effect. Margolis continues, "We keep the same editor all the way through. We hire the editor in California, and bring him here, in order to insure perfect continuity."

Ray Klausen, the designer for the 1994 show, illustrates how involved his process is: "As soon as the producers have a theme, I come aboard. I confer with the musical director and the choreog-

Mary Ann Mobley and husband Gary Collins and Mary Clancy Collins.

rapher and we decide on colors, lighting, and space."

For the 1994 production, the scenery was built in seven different shops in Los Angeles, Dallas, Washington, D.C., Philadelphia, and Atlantic City. Klausen traveled to each site to coordinate set creation. All the pieces were shipped to Atlantic City and put together like a giant jigsaw puzzle. Klausen arrived in Atlantic City about three weeks ahead of the production crew to begin assembling the sets. "The wonderful thing about the show is it's about beautiful women so the scenery becomes a jewel box setting for these lovely women to shine in."

The same amount of effort, attention to detail, and concentration extends to every aspect of the television show. Everyone on the team — writers, musical director, choreographer, producers, and technicians — works for months to create a show. This is a far cry from the one-day camera availability of the 1950s. Today there are very few restrictions on television involvement. Director Jeff Margolis takes advantage of the latest available technology to bring an exciting, modern television show to millions of viewers without sacrificing the quality of the live presentation in Convention Center.

According to Tom Boles, executive in charge of production, today's telecast uses eight miles of electrical cable, one thousand lighting instruments, and enough electricity to power forty-eight homes for twenty-four hours with all appliances running. It takes two computer systems just to run the lighting on the show, three miles of video cable, two miles of audio cable, and nine television cameras.

While technological advances have changed the face of the Miss America Pageant, its stated purpose and goals remain. High quality contestants, striving to achieve these lofty goals and represent the American ideal, keep the viewing audience tuned in.

Top: During the early days of television coverage, huge heat generating lights were mounted on one rail above the stage. Today, hundreds of small computer-controlled units are placed in multiple grids.

Above: Director Jeff Margolis, focused and alert in the control room during the 1994 telecast.

Leonard

*Leonard C. Horn —
creating a new image*

"**P**ROGRESS. That's what we're all about," Leonard Horn says. "Either move ahead, or die standing still."

The evolution of the Pageant from a bathing beauty contest to the major event it is today has certainly been a journey of moving ahead, but at a snail's pace. Not that the Pageant didn't try. It folded when the original gimmick died, and was resurrected after a lot of changes as a "Showman's Jubilee" in the thirties. Toward the end of that decade, it began evolving into the forerunner of today's Pageant — though it was the forties before Pageant officials bothered to copyright the name Miss America.

Then came the war years. War was good for the Pageant. It provided a diversion. Something already identifiably American to millions of servicemen. Miss America became a welcome symbol of home — like Mom and

LEONARD C. HORN

"The public had a perception of the Pageant that was stuck in a time warp. It was my job to change that perception to reflect today's modern, sophisticated young women."

ROSEMARY LA PLANCHE
MISS AMERICA 1941

MARILYN BUFERD
MISS AMERICA 1946

YOLANDE BETBEZE
MISS AMERICA 1951

*When Bert Parks asked me
how I would cope if I was
walking down the runway
in swimsuit and broke a
heel, I said I would take off
both shoes as I didn't think
it very natural to wear heels
with swimsuit anyway. Wow!
Thirty-four years later, they
heard me . . . those slow
wheels of progress!"*

— NANCY FLEMING
MISS AMERICA 1961

With their white dresses and long gloves, contestants projected a debutante image in 1957.

apple pie. It's true that contestants did a lot of posturing in swimsuits, copying the cheesecake pinups of Hollywood glamour queens, but that's what the GIs wanted. Besides, they always had their chaperones, and they performed community services, selling war bonds and visiting veterans' hospitals. The public loved Miss America in the forties.

Thank God for television. It gave the Pageant a much needed boost in the 1950s. And the Pageant gave something to television, as well. Along with Milton Berle and Arthur Godfrey, the images of pretty young girls beamed from Atlantic City helped make television our national passion and Bert Parks' singing "There She Is" our last good-bye to summer. Clearly, television and the Pageant were made for each other.

There must have been something reassuring about turning on that set every September and seeing what was basically the same show year after year. By the time the sixties rolled around, the world was changing a lot faster than most people could handle. The Pageant was a constant. And people liked it for that. For a while.

Then something happened to television. Perhaps nothing in American experience ever projected as distorted an image of this country as did television. It was white. Families were white. Communities were white. So was television — from "Leave it to Beaver" to "My Three Sons," "Father Knows Best" to "The Dick Van Dyke show," "The Andy Griffith Show" to "The Waltons" . . . to "The Miss America Pageant."

That was before Vanessa Williams. Before satellites and cable offered home viewers choices they had never dreamed possible. Before black children would learn that black was beautiful. That's when television began bringing the sights and signs of America into millions of homes: Vietnam, civil rights clashes, armed troopers escorting black children to school, women protesting. And that's when the Pageant began to catch up.

"Not that the program wasn't terrific — it was great," Horn explains. "We made a lot of changes over the years, but the public had a perception that was stuck in a time warp. We had to articulate our vision." So while the Pageant had been making changes all along, the changes came so slowly that the general perception was that the Pageant hadn't changed at all!

That's a perception Leonard Horn changed when he became chief executive officer in 1987. "I discovered my vision was the same as all of my predecessors. Certainly, Lenora Slaughter had a vision, and Albert A. Marks had a vision. But it wasn't getting across to the public, and I had to do something about that."

The first thing Horn did was to commission a group of studies to discover exactly what the public perception of the program was. And the results were devastating. As he met with various sponsors, the news got worse. "They told me Miss America was a turn-off instead of a turn-on," Horn says. "It panicked me."

Pageant officials had reason to panic. In 1986 the Pageant had a problem selling the show; something that had never happened in Pageant history. When the television producer arrived in Atlantic City nine days before air, he received a message that several clients had backed out and there were three or four unsold spots on the show. An independent sales promoter was brought in, and at the last minute all spots were sold.

The proliferation of new channels and networks, the soaring increase in VCRS, and better and less controversial ways of advertising products, coupled with increased competition with other pageants and a faulty perception by the public of the Pageant itself, forced Pageant officials to make changes. Costs were going up, and ratings were going down. This fact gave longtime sponsors pause. Regardless of their personal attachments to the Pageant, they had to get results for their dollars.

"I basically had to do five things immediately," Horn says. "Put the Pageant on a solid financial base, change the way the contestants present themselves, modernize the television show, reorient the judges as to what they should be looking for, and convince sponsors of the value of the program."

The first thing Horn did was change the name of the Pageant from The Miss America Pageant to The Miss America Organization. Under the umbrella of The Miss America Organization is the Pageant, the Scholarship Fund, and The Miss America Foundation.

NANCY FLEMING
MISS AMERICA 1961

REBECCA KING
MISS AMERICA 1974

Leonard Horn and Karen Aarons, cell phones in hand, keep tabs on every aspect of the production during Pageant week.

No one expected the green-eyed beauty who performed a sexy South Seas dance for her talent to talk about the hospice program, but Kaye Lani Rae Rafko, an oncology nurse from Michigan who won the crown in 1987, did just that during the interview portion of the competition. She promoted her cause during her year of service and the idea of the platform issue for all future contestants was born.

The Miss America Foundation was developed by Horn to expand scholarship opportunities beyond contestants. For example, the Foundation awards a $25,000 scholarship fund to the current Miss America's college or university to help non-contestants continue their studies. The Foundation also sponsors the Miss America Woman's Achievement Award, a $10,000 prize given to the woman who was most inspirational to the reigning Miss America during her year of service.

Horn then appointed a women's advisory committee, composed of prominent professional women, to advise officials on women's issues, program development, and to offer guidelines on the activities Miss America pursues during her year. In addition, Horn initiated sponsor-funded special scholarships, which will be discussed in chapter seven.

A full-scale public relations effort spread the word across the country at the local and state level that Miss America was going to be perceived as more than a pretty face. That's when Gretchen Carlson decided she had a shot at becoming Miss America.

When Carlson heard about Leonard Horn's vision of a Miss America who would not only be beautiful and talented, but who had brains and ambition as well, she decided the time was right for her. "I had been a serious classical violinist my whole life, and dreamed of performing in Carnegie Hall. I had studied at Oxford University in England, and was working on a degree from Stanford. When my mother and I read about Leonard Horn's vision for the

GRETCHEN CARLSON
MISS AMERICA 1989

Nan Roman, vice president of the National Alliance to End Homelessness, accepts the Miss America Woman of Achievement Award from Miss America 1994, Kimberly Aiken.

Pageant we believed if I worked hard enough, I had a very good chance at being the Miss America Horn was talking about," Carlson says.

And she was right. The first classical violinist to win the title, Carlson is now a television anchor/reporter who says that being Miss America was a "phenomenal" experience. "Today's Miss America has the opportunity to be a positive role model and to have a real impact on society, and that's something the Pageant can be proud of," she says.

Certainly Carlson was not the first Miss America with ambition and brains. Becky King, Miss America 1974, recalls, "Although Miss America contestants had a long history of fostering college education, and although many contestants were college graduates before me, I was the first who said I wanted to go to law school, and that I was in it for the money. Al Marks was appalled, but I told him being Miss America was a job. Now young women are told to think of entering the competition as applying for a job — the job of being Miss America."

But the public held a different vision of Miss America, an image that was hard to shake, cultivated through the years of negative publicity. Horn's job was to change all that.

Long after the on-stage question was dropped from the television show, the public's memories remained of a time when a contestant might be asked what she would do if the heel of her shoe broke during the show, or if she liked Bermuda shorts. Some were worse. Mary Ann Mobley, Miss America 1959, was asked what she would talk about on a date, and Phyllis George talked about her pet crab! Not exactly the kind of questions symbolic of brains and ambition. Especially when contestants' measurements were part of the package.

Karen Aarons recalls, "When I came in ten years ago, almost the entire focus was on Miss America, and it was my goal to make The Miss America Organization and the general public know that there were forty-nine very accomplished young women in Atlantic City. One of the first things I did was ask Al Marks to take out the measurements, which he did." This was a step in the right direction, but Pageant officials felt something more was needed.

Until 1988, Miss America was defined as the all-around ideal young American woman: attractive, ambitious, bright, wholesome. "What I did was add another dimension to that definition," Horn explains.

It all started with Kaye Lani Rae Rafko, Miss America 1988. Rafko, who performed a Hawaiian-Tahitian hula for her talent, was full of surprises. No one expected the green-eyed beauty who wore a revealing red sequined dress in her state pageant to talk about the hospice program on the national telecast. But Rafko was a nurse who dealt with the terminally ill, and even though she was advised the subject was a downer, she insisted on promoting the hospice program whenever possible. The public responded to her, and

Deborah Bryant, Miss America 1966, with her court of honor.

Leonard Horn got an idea. Why not have all contestants select a compelling civic or social issue and promote that issue on the show?

Today the judges look for a woman who has a sincere sensitivity to some of the troublesome issues in the world and a willingness to work towards solutions in some defined way. To attract qualified contestants, Horn added a requirement that each contestant have a specific platform issue, and that she be willing to promote that issue during her year of service.

Karen Aarons adds, "Before 1988 the Pageant was very introverted. We had a wonderful television show that drew sponsors all the time, but as the years passed there was more and more need for the Pageant to come out and say what we stand for, and that is why the platform requirement is so good. That's the biggest change."

The late Pageant president Adrian Phillips once remarked that everything that has happened to the Pageant has been the result of something that came before. "It comes by evolving and it disappears by evolving."

Leonard Horn calls it a natural evolution. "This duckling of a program which was born under the auspices of Lenora Slaughter and was nurtured and grown to adult life under Al Marks, is now ready to be turned into a swan."

Horn might be right. No one can say the Pageant is just another beauty contest. It's now the largest scholarship program in the world, and it uses the name Miss America to promote and support meaningful programs.

Chapter Five

Strength Through Crisis

You have to have a positive attitude, you must believe in your dreams, you must face obstacles, you must be willing to work hard, and you have to build a support team. That's my star five point platform, and that's what it takes to endure.

— HEATHER WHITESTONE
MISS AMERICA 1995

Strength

When Heather Whitestone dreamed up her STARS Platform as a message for school children, she was a visible personification of that doctrine: she was deaf and she had succeeded in spite of that handicap. What she could not have known was that the Miss America Pageant had been practicing that philosophy since its beginning.

Perhaps Pageant officials never articulated it that way; theirs was more of a "pick yourself up, dust yourself off, and start all over again," approach. And it worked. Overcoming obstacles and standing by its convictions have played big parts in the history and success of the Pageant.

MASTER OF CEREMONIES BERT PARKS

During Bert's years as host, the on-stage question was usually frivolous in nature but was, nonetheless, part of the judging process.

Gary Collins, Phyllis George
and Bert Parks together at the
Pageant's 70th anniversary show.

Regis Philbin and Kathie Lee
Gifford utlimately replaced
Gary Collins as hosts of the
Miss America telecast.

For instance, Miss America 1943, Jean Bartel, refused to pose in a bathing suit after she was chosen. "I wanted to focus on a singing/acting career," she explains today. "It wasn't the image I was trying to present." Bartel's rebellion apparently didn't offend Catalina; they continued to sponsor the event, Miss America was still crowned in a swimsuit, and subsequent winners continued to model swimsuits during their years.

Then in 1948, at the behest of the Hostess Committee, Lenora Slaughter decided Miss America would be crowned in an evening gown instead of a swimsuit. E.W. Stewart, president of Catalina, Inc., manufacturers of the official swimsuits worn by the contestants, gave his wholehearted approval and continued as one of the two national sponsors of the Scholarship Foundation. (Actually, Miss America 1933, Marian Bergeron, had been crowned in a gown, but that year the Pageant was run under a management that was subsequently discredited, and the precedent wasn't mentioned in subsequent press releases.)

The Pageant, consistently embarrassed by the bathing suit, had been chipping away at its importance since the earliest pageants. Slaughter hoped to upgrade the image of Miss America and downgrade the importance of the swimsuit by crowning Miss America in an evening gown. The result was the

1 9 8 3   P A G E A N T   R E U N I O N

L–R Top row: Mary Ann Mobley, Miss America 1959; Gary Collins; Nancy Fleming, Miss America 1961.
Middle row: Rebecca King, Miss America 1974; Debra Maffett, Miss America 1983; Jean Bartel, Miss America 1943.
Bottom row: Dorothy Benham, Miss America 1977; Lynda Mead, Miss America 1960; Judith Ford, Miss America 1969.

NANCY FLEMING
MISS AMERICA 1961

Nancy is married to television personality Jim Lange and lives in California where her interests include garden design, home renovation, and travel. Her daughter, Ingrid Johnson, is a psychologist, and her son, Steig Johnson, is studying for his doctorate in anthropology. After the Pageant she enjoyed a long career as a lecturer and television personality and today produces and hosts the television show "Sewing Today." Sewing was her talent when she competed at the Miss America Pageant; the sewing show is a continuation of a lifelong interest.

66

The negative side of winning the crown was that I thought I was just lucky and didn't really deserve it. It took a lot of years and self-examination to realize my winning was based on intelligence, diligence, and a strong work ethic. I believe that the Pageant has survived because it has developed a screening process that encourages bright, motivated young women to participate. In my era, women were still being defined by who they married; today's contestant has her own agenda. The most telling change is the inclusion of the interview in the scoring process, and while the 'platform' may seem contrived to some people, at least it gives the winner a focus that will continue for the entire year.

99

miss america speaks

threat of a boycott by photographers who wanted and needed that traditional cheesecake sure seller — fifty beautiful girls in bathing suits showing off their shapely legs.

The afternoon of the show, press photographers packed their cameras, newsreel men dismantled their platforms and lights. Pageant directors knew a crisis had been reached. Did the event have sufficient significance to warrant coverage as news — not cheesecake? Could the Pageant survive a news blackout?

The standoff lasted only a few hours. Pageant officials refused to back down, and when news editors across the country got word of what was happening, they ordered their reporters and photographers to return to the Pageant. As showtime neared, a dramatic transformation took place inside Convention Hall. Back came the cameras, the newsreel platforms, and the bright spotlights. The next day, the new Miss America, BeBe Shopp, saw her face smiling back at her from the front pages of newspapers from coast-to-coast, evening gown and all.

It's become part of Pageant folklore that this milestone in reshaping the Pageant image was blessed by the very members of the press corps who began the brouhaha. The story goes that, hat in hand, each approached Lenora Slaughter after the show and said, "You were right. Now I would be proud to have my own daughter take part in your contest." That wasn't the end of it, however. When Yolande Betbeze, Miss America 1951, refused to pose in a swimsuit during her year's reign, Catalina threw up its hands and said, "enough!" This time, Catalina's president demanded that she be forced to go on with the tour as planned or be disqualified.

Once again, Pageant officials stood firm. They believed in their dream: that Miss America personify dignity, talent, self-reliance, and wholesomeness. The Pageant backed Betbeze and Catalina backed out. They withdrew their sponsorship and started a rival pageant, Miss Universe.

Although no one can explain how a gimmick to extend the summer season metamorphosed into an American tradition, the Miss America Pageant is right up there with the World Series and the Rose Bowl Parade. But the Pageant became something personal, the individual and collective property of the American public — something they could satirize, criticize, make fun of, or pretend they never watched.

**Nancy Fleming with husband Jim Lange
and son Steig and daughter Ingrid.**

But it was still "their" Miss America Pageant. So when Pageant officials tried to drop Bernie Wayne's "There She Is, Miss America" from its music repertoire, and when Bert Parks was replaced — both indelible fixtures of the Pageant since 1955 — America was up in arms.

Glenn Osser recalls Parks' beginnings with the Pageant: "Pierson Mapes, head of advertising for Philco, and Paul Whiteman, head of music at ABC, were having lunch at a restaurant adjacent to the ice skating rink in Rockefeller Center when Bert Parks walked in. Whiteman said to Mapes, 'That's the guy you should get to host Miss America,' and that's how Bert Parks came to the Pageant."

Parks was not an unknown. He was host of a popular television show, "Stop The Music," and he had all the qualities that would endear him to millions of viewers: folksy charm, talent, and a vaudevillian's genius at turning pratfalls into comedy. He was either hated or loved — and clearly more loved than hated.

After twenty-five years, the sponsors began pressuring Al Marks to replace Parks. Leonard Horn recalls, "They thought he was too old and too corny.

Legs! Legs! Legs! Catalina supplied the swimsuits, and to the delight of many 1940s photographers, contestants supplied the cheesecake, a representation disdained by Pageant officials. Crowning the winner in an evening gown instead of a swimsuit lost the Pageant a major sponsor, but succeeded in polishing the Pageant's tarnished image, garnering new respect for Miss America.

JACQUELYN MAYER
MISS AMERICA 1963

Jacquelyn and her husband, John Townsend, live in Pennsylvania where they own a Standardbred horse farm. Son Bill and daughter Kelly are both out of college and are pursuing business careers. Jackie suffered a stroke in 1970 which left her paralyzed and without speech. Today she is ninety percent recovered. She is a founding member and on the executive board of the National Stroke Association, is on the Advisory Council of the National Institute of Neurological Disorders and Stroke, and serves on the board of the American Heart Association.

66

The only negative of being Miss America is that sometimes people have much higher expectations than you can deliver. The positive side is that because of the celebrity of the crown I have become the lay spokesperson for two leading neurological disorder associations. The Pageant has endured because I truly believe people are looking for female role models. Today, Miss America is a woman of the '90s who uses the intelligence and personality that has stamped all Miss Americas to educate, motivate, and to facilitate social programs. I would like to see the scholarship increased to keep up with rising college costs. I loved every minute of being Miss America and have maintained a thirty-year friendship with fellow contestants; they will be part of my life forever!

99

R–L: Jacquelyn Mayer, son Bill, daughter Kelly, husband John Townsend.

miss america speaks

They wanted someone who could create more excitement and bring a more youthful prospective to the show, and after resisting for a long time, Marks gave in."

The public's reaction was completely unexpected; they were outraged. Johnny Carson took up the cause and began a letter-writing campaign on his late night show. Thousands of letters poured into Pageant offices. "We were shocked at the reaction," Horn says.

It was, perhaps, the manner in which Parks was dismissed that flamed public passion. A letter was sent to Parks' home in Connecticut while he was on his way to Florida. The news was somehow leaked to the press, and Parks read about his dismissal in the newspapers. "Bert was devastated," says Edna Osser, a close personal friend. "It was a very unfortunate chain of circumstances," Leonard Horn explains. "We never meant to appear so uncaring."

Things got worse. Ron Ely, who was selected to replace Parks, didn't click with the public. While this might have had something to do with loyalty to Bert Parks, Horn believes there was more to it. "One of the reasons why Bert was so terrific for so many years was that he recognized that the stars of the show are the fifty contestants, and the job of the host is to make them as comfortable as possible while moving the show along. Ron Ely seemed to be more interested in promoting himself, and the public must have sensed that."

The public continued to call for Parks return. After only two years, Ely was replaced — but by Gary Collins, not Bert Parks.

"Gary brought a certain stability to the show," Horn says. "He looked like he belonged up on that stage with the contestants. He projected stability, fineness, and culture, and while it lasted he was good for the show." After eight years, Horn decided that, while Gary's qualities saw the show through some rough times, stability, fineness, and culture weren't enough. He was looking for excitement, and that's when the popular television personalities Regis Philbin and Kathie Lee Gifford replaced Collins. As when Ely was replaced, hardly a word was heard from the public; apparently no host or hostess captured American hearts as Bert Parks did.

Two years after Bert Parks was replaced, the Pageant dropped the familiar strains of "There She Is," which had accompanied the newly crowned winner on her walk down the runway at Convention Hall for twenty-seven years.

"The composer, Bernie Wayne, wanted too much money for the performing rights," Al Marks said at the time. Under a fifteen-year contract signed in 1968, Wayne was paid $1,166.67 a year for the once-a-year use of his song. It became a kind of trademark of the Pageant.

Any other show would die for an instantly recognizable theme, but Marks was firm. Although he declined to say how much Mr. Wayne wanted for a renewed fifteen-year contract, he noted that it was "well up into the six figures — an amount that was far beyond our reach."

"Before 'There She Is,' we used to play something everybody knew, usually something rather innocuous that was easy to walk to," Glen Osser recalls. "After they dropped 'There She Is' we used two other songs, 'Miss America, You're Beautiful' and 'Look At Her, She's A Miss America.'" But Wayne's melody was part of the tradition, and the public wanted it back.

According to the late Bernie Wayne, he didn't start out to create a tradition. "I just sat down in my office and tried to put myself in the place of the girl walking down the runway," he once told a reporter. Although both the producer and music conductor loved the song, Bob Russell, who was the emcee of the show at the time, insisted on using his own compositions. But when Pierson Mapes, who was a guest at a party in New York where Bernie Wayne was playing, heard "There She Is," he knew it was absolutely right for Miss America.

The song was first sung by Johnny Desmond who sang it to Lee Meriwether, the reigning queen, on a Philco Playhouse television show in 1955, and Bert Parks sang it for the first time a few weeks later when Sharon Kay Ritchie, Miss America 1956, was crowned queen.

It was sung to every Miss America until 1982, when Marks and Wayne came to blows over money. "I was surprised and disappointed," Wayne said in a *New York Times* interview that year. But Marks had a different view. "I am noted for making decisions and getting hung with them. But after the hullabaloo about Mr. Parks, I think people are tired of making so much about nothing. We're doing our best by the contestants — they're the stars, not the

Left: Bert Parks with contestants in 1958.

Top: Bert Parks with Vonda Kay Van Dyke, Miss America 1965.

Above: Bert Parks and composer Bernie Wayne.

Al Marks above and at right (fourth from left, bottom row) with board of directors in 1974.

music or the emcee. The music is not essential. It's used for twenty seconds at the end of the telecast, and it's not that important."

This time Marks was wrong. And without disclosing the new financial arrangements with Wayne, the force of public opinion prevailed, an agreement was reached, and a tradition was preserved.

A far bigger crisis faced the Pageant in 1968. That year, Lincoln Park in Chicago was turned in a bloody battlefield when police clashed with antiwar protesters during the Democratic Convention. In Washington, civil rights advocates picketed the White House. The word "hippie" had recently been added to American idioms, miniskirts were the hot new fashion, the sexual revolution was sending shockwaves through the country, and women were entering a new phase of self-awareness and self-determination.

The first Saturday after Labor Day in 1968 saw soft breezes, gently lapping waves, and warm temperatures at the Jersey shore. Inside Convention Center, rehearsal for the Pageant went on with its usual last minute panic — torn swimsuit straps and missed television cues — nothing extraordinary. Outside on the boardwalk, however, two events were taking place that would shake up the Pageant: Women armed with a giant bathing beauty puppet threw girdles, bras, hair curlers, false eyelashes, and anything else that smacked of "enslavement" into a "freedom trash can" and picketed the Miss America Pageant, while a few blocks from Convention Hall, a Black Miss America Pageant was capturing the attention of newsmen and television crews.

Saundra Williams, that year's Miss Black America, commented on the

women's protest. "They're expressing freedom, I guess," she said. "To each his own."

Pageant officials remember the incident differently. Al Marks dismissed the incident as "a number of wild-eyed females out of New York who needed publicity," and Leonard Horn said, "They had no effect on the Pageant whatsoever." Oddly enough, they were both right and wrong.

According to Robin Morgan, author of *The World of a Woman,* the 1968 women's demonstration against the Miss America Pageant was the first major action of the current wave of feminism in the United States. She wrote, "We came, we saw, and if we didn't conquer, we learned. And other women learned that we existed; the week before the demonstration there had been thirty women at the New York Radical Women meeting; the week after, there were approximately a hundred and fifty."

What Pageant officials didn't know at the time was that one of their own, that same fiery rebel who spoke out against racism in the Pageant and refused to pose in a swimsuit, Yolande Betbeze, was one of the organizers of the event. "We picketed the Pageant because it was a good vehicle to get noticed,"

Betbeze says. "Besides, it was time for the Pageant to take a good look at itself."

Sharon Kay Ritchie, Miss America 1956, has a different memory. "I appeared on many talk shows with those women. Invariably, they were rude, angry, and obnoxious on the subject of beauty and the rewards for beauty. They just didn't realize that it's very difficult to want to buy something from an angry person."

The effects on the Pageant aren't easily quantified. Ellen Plum, former chairman of the hostess committee recalls, "I remember feeling at the time

Donna Axum and husband Bryan Whitworth.

miss america speaks

that we were one step ahead of the women's movement since we had been giving women scholarships for years, but that the movement probably prodded the Pageant into making changes. For instance, I was the first woman to become a member of the board outside of the head of the hostess committee who is automatically a member, and I believe the women's movement had something to do with that."

The intervening twenty-plus years have seen the feminist protests on both state and national levels become as much a tradition as the Pageant itself. The most notable was the successful infiltration by a feminist "contestant" at the 1988 Miss California state pageant in San Diego who pulled a banner reading "Pageants Hurt All Women" from her bra on live TV.

"We didn't understand them and they didn't understand us back in 1968," says Leonard Horn. "But the Women's Movement helped effectuate tremendous changes in the lives of women and it was inevitable that we change our focus to accommodate those changes."

Jana Talton, a staff member at *Ms. Magazine,* sums it up this way: "I find it disingenuous at best, of those associated with the Miss America Pageant, to dismiss the significance of the 1968 protest, just as though the many changes instituted in pageants in these past years had not been brought about precisely in response to what is so passively described as the 'changing role of women in society.'" Well, at least they agree on something.

Despite the wide scope of this crisis, the greatest threat to the reputation and stability of the Pageant was yet to come. Ironically, it came at a time when the Pageant had made one of its greatest breakthroughs, crowning both a black Miss America and a black First Runner-Up. The year Vanessa Williams was crowned, the roof caved in.

Just eight weeks short of concluding her one-year reign, word reached Al Marks that nude pictures of Vanessa Williams were about to be published in *Penthouse Magazine.* Williams assured Marks that the pictures were semi-nude: "a pearl here, and a drape there, that sort of thing," and Marks decided he could accommodate that. He immediately convened a meeting of his executive committee to decide what to do. "Board members first thought we'd just have to live with it, that we just couldn't take away her crown," Leonard Horn recalls. "To which I immediately responded, 'you're wrong.' I said that if you do not take the crown away or ask her to resign, this program will die." When the pictures were delivered to the meeting, everyone went into shock. They were graphic combinations of lesbian shots and full frontal nudity. Obviously Williams was talking about a different set of pictures. "The minute each person in the room saw the pictures it became crystal clear that in the interests of the Pageant she would be asked to resign," Horn says.

Everyone agreed that Vanessa Williams was a great Miss America who had made a mistake. But they had to decide who was more important: Vanessa or all future Pageant contestants? They had to consider the sponsors who put up millions of dollars. They had to weigh the national impression versus her welfare and the Pageant's welfare. They had to consider the implications of being labeled racist. "Somewhere, the Lord smiled upon us," Al Marks was heard to remark. "We had a black First Runner-Up, so charges of racism were ridiculous, and besides, when Roy White from the NAACP saw the pictures he agreed with our decision."

When Williams' lawyer protested, Horn reminded him that there were going to be thousands of mothers who would not allow their daughters to enter the program if Miss America was allowed to pose in the nude. Williams was given seventy-two hours to think it over, and when she asked what would happen if she didn't resign, Horn answered "I don't know." The following Monday, at a press conference in New York, Williams resigned.

L–R: Miss New Jersey, Suzette Charles; Miss New York, Vanessa Williams; and Miss Connecticut, Dakeita Vanderburg, frolic in the surf during Pageant week 1983. Miss Williams and Miss Charles both hold the title for the year 1984.

"I really didn't know what would happen," says Horn. "In my first year as CEO I was questioned by the press whether it made any difference if a contestant had a premarital sexual history, and I told them it was none of our business, as long as they were not promiscuous. I received tons of irate letters that said we shouldn't lower our standards just because society did."

"That's what we were confronted with in Vanessa's case. If those pictures had taken place two decades before, there would have been no question that they were immoral." Horn explains. "Today, it isn't so simple. The world has changed, and we are confronted with the question of what is and isn't moral in today's society."

To prepare themselves for possible future controversies, Horn initiated a board discussion of how the Pageant should uphold its standards in today's society.

"The second thing we did right at that time was to refuse to debate what happened," says Horn. "We maintained our dignity, and in the intervening years, she restored her dignity."

Anything is Possible

In facing my own life's challenges, I have discovered a unique approach that I call "STARS: Success Through Action and Realization (of your dreamS)." The five points of a star remind me that the essential elements to achieving success are:

- ★ *have a positive attitude*
- ★ *believe in your dream*
- ★ *face your obstacles*
- ★ *work hard*
- ★ *build a support team*

As I travel this country in my role as Miss America, I will communicate the STARS approach to our nation's youth. I will teach them, through word and deed, the value of setting high goals, working hard, and achieving their dreams and ambitions.

As a living example of a challenged person who has used a STARS approach to succeed, I will extend my hand to anyone in need of encouragement and love. I will ask them not to imitate me, but rather to believe in themselves and the power of their spirit.

It is my goal to motivate all young people who are deaf or hard of hearing to pursue a broad range of communication and educational options, helping them choose those which best reflect their goals.

I will invite young people with disabilities to join me in reaching out to the non-disabled world — without fear or concern — to tear down the barriers of acceptance by demonstrating that their lives are about their *abilities* not their *disabilities*. And I will encourage all young people facing challenges to confront their obstacles with determination and confidence.

Finally, I will challenge those who influence youth to work hard at creating the proper environment where disabled and non-disabled young people can establish their own identities and build self-esteem.

I will commit myself to these young people and countless others, speaking out for those who cannot speak out for themselves. I will believe in their dreams. And I will always be the very first member of their support team.

Excerpts from the platform essay of
Heather Whitestone, Miss America 1995

HEATHER WHITESTONE
MISS AMERICA 1995

Chapter Six
The Miss America Family

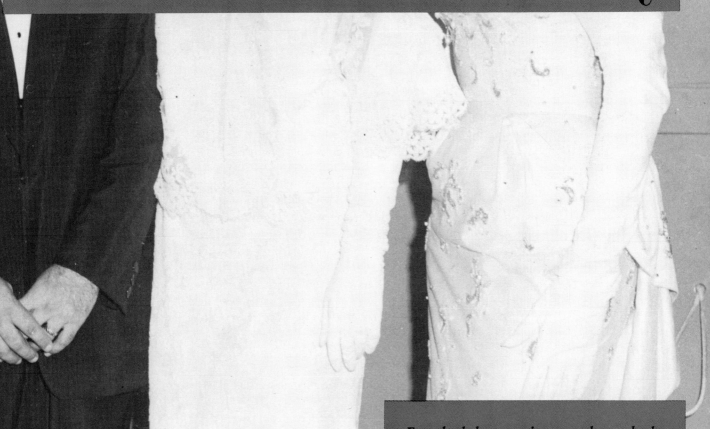

Everybody loves a winner, and everybody loves being on a winning team.

— BILL CALIGARI
*National Production Manager
The Miss America Organization*

Family

OCTOBER 7, 1994, is a perfect day in Conneaut, Ohio. The sun glistens off Lake Erie, trees are ablaze with the golden, fiery hues of fall, high school football fields are bursting with enthusiasm, young boys are skipping down the street on the way home from Little League, and Halloween pumpkins and corn husks decorate front porches. With its wide lawns, shade trees, neat houses, and covered bridges, the town is a Norman Rockwell illustration come to life.

Nestled snugly along the shores of Lake Erie, right at the tip of the northeast corner of the state, Conneaut covers a relatively large area — twenty-eight square miles — though its population of 15,000 is comparatively small.

MISS AMERICA FAMILY

Bert Parks joins Miss Americas and former contestants in "Kraft Music Hall Special" in 1971.

It's a very special day in Conneaut. It's just twenty days since a new Miss America was crowned in Atlantic City, and it's already time for the eighth annual Miss Conneaut Scholarship Pageant. Preparations for this night began the day after the Ohio State Pageant, held in June 1994. That's when local pageant directors placed ads in the *Ohio Pageant Newsletter,* local newspapers, and at high schools and local colleges, asking those interested in competing to contact local officials.

Linda Wires, a full-time school teacher and the Miss Conneaut executive director, volunteers her time to organize this local pageant. So does Anthony Maukonen, master of ceremonies, who, when he is not hosting this pageant, can be found working as an accountant. The pageant's director/producer/choreographer, Mary Murtha, has her own dance studio. "We have a core group of about ten volunteers," Wires says. "Then as we get close to show time, we just beg our friends and families to help out, and they do."

Greg Sweet, owner of Conneaut's Chevrolet dealership, donates the $2,100 scholarship fund, while other local townspeople and businessmen make additional scholarship donations. Other local businesses contribute services such as tuxedos, flowers, hotel accommodations, food, and decorations.

"We need donations," Linda Wires explains. "We have to pay for use of the auditorium, sound, lights, printing, and sets." Anthony Maukonen adds,

The road to the crown begins in small towns and cities all across the country. Contestants (left) in Coney Island, N.Y., compete in swimsuits in 1928.

Above: Miss Dallas (top), late 1920s and Miss Des Moines 1935.

"We run a raffle, have bake sales, and depend on ticket sales to cover our expenses."

Lenora Slaughter began using local Jaycees to organize pageants in the thirties. The Chamber of Commerce lent an air of respectability to the contest, and it shifted the financial responsibility for local pageants away from the national office.

All that has changed. In the past, many Jaycee and civic organizations used the Pageant as a means to raise funds for their own programs. "Funds raised through any pageant must be used to further benefit that pageant, and when the Jaycees did not share that point of view and insisted that such money go back into their general funds, the system was changed," Karen Aarons explains. As of 1994, only the Louisiana Pageant was still under the auspices of the Jaycees.

So how does one get to sponsor a local pageant? According to Karen Aarons, any interested group must first contact the state organization. If there is no other local in that city, the state director will instruct the group to incorporate as a nonprofit organization, elect a board of directors, decide where the pageant will be held, and determine the origination of the scholarship fund. When all criteria are met, the organization will be awarded a franchise. This organization might be a loosely collected group of people, or an offshoot of some already established civic organization.

When Lea Mack, Miss Ohio 1994, competed in her local, it was sponsored by the Pickerington Ohio Fourth of July Committee, which was affiliated with

Marcia Hyland (center, bottom) producer of the Miss New Jersey Pageant pictured with the 1994–95 contestants.

the City of Pickerington, and by Youth Excellence and Service Productions, a nonprofit civic group.

"The basic thing is that the funds raised through the local pageant be used for the benefit of contestants — whether it be to prepare them for the next stage of competition, to give them opportunities to network, to fund travel expenses, or award scholarships," Aarons says.

Volunteerism. That's the bedrock of the entire Miss America Organization. All across the country, at approximately 2,400 local pageants held at various times of the year, thousands of volunteers devote time and energy to usher the more than 70,000 contestants through the pageants, and the winners on to the State competitions. From these contestants, fifty will make it to Atlantic City, and just one will become Miss America.

This night no one is dwelling on those seemingly impossible odds. Here in Conneaut, the chances of winning are one in thirteen; when the winner competes in the Ohio State Pageant, the odds will be one in thirty-six; and when the winner of the State Pageant competes in Atlantic City, those odds increase to one in fifty. But Miss America, whoever she is, is selected from towns and small cities like Conneaut all around the country. This is where it all begins.

At 8:00 P.M., while October daylight still lingers outdoors, the inside of Conneaut's high school auditorium sparkles with light and color. The room is jammed with enthusiastic parents, sponsors, supporters, and friends. On stage, silver stars hang from the ceiling, appearing to glitter from a deep blue sky. A Disney-like castle, complete with dragons and cardboard prince and princess, suggests the theme, "Dreams can come true."

Lea Mack, fresh from making "top ten" in the Atlantic City Pageant just a few short weeks before, is on hand to entertain and co-host the show.

The opening production number, performed by the Wildfire Dance Team, a local dance troupe, sets the mood. Afterwards, the format follows that of the Miss America Pageant. What is called the "Parade of States" in Atlantic City is here a parade of just thirteen contestants from Ashtabula County and surrounding areas. The contestants compete in swimsuit, evening wear, and talent, and answer an on-stage question.

(L–R) Shawna Corder, Miss Conneaut 1994, Robin Bobal, winner of the Miss Conneaut 1995 Pageant, and Lea Mack, Miss Ohio 1994–95.

Last year's Miss Conneaut and Lea Mack provide entertainment during breaks for costume changes. The panel of judges are introduced, the on-stage question is asked, and then it's all over.

The winner, Robin Bobal, who played an intricate Chopin piano composition, is a premed student at Case Western Reserve University. She has previously competed and won two local Ohio pageants; this will be her third trip to Mansfield to compete in the Ohio State Pageant.

The winner receives $1,000, with the remaining money divided among the runners-up. "I won a total of about $3,000 just being in locals and the Miss Ohio State," Bobal explains. "But it hasn't quite covered my expenses for clothes, travel, and music preparation, so far."

The decision to compete barefoot during the swimsuit competition in Atlantic City has not filtered down to this local pageant yet, so each contestant makes the walk down Conneaut's twenty-foot runway in high heels. "Wearing a swimsuit and walking in high heels before a crowd of people was awkward at first, but I'm getting used to it," the new Miss Conneaut says. "Anyway, it has more relevance now because now it's about physical fitness."

It's no accident that the local pageant follows rigid guidelines. A kit is sent from the national office to every local and state pageant in the country to insure that all pageants are run according to exactly the same rules. The length of time for interviews, the time allowed for talent, the weighting of all the areas of competition, the number of judges, the eligibility rules for contestants, and the eligibility rules for judges are all determined by the national board of directors of the Miss America Organization, and are carefully followed throughout the country.

The state pageants, which must be completed by the end of the second week in July — two months before the national telecast — vary in number

depending upon the size of the state and the number of participants. It's axiomatic that small states, such as Rhode Island, have few locals and few contestants, while large states, such as Texas, Ohio, and California, might have up to sixty local pageants with dozens of contestants.

New Jersey is an exception. Though small in size, it held thirty-three local pageants in small towns across the state in 1994. The state pageant was held in the convention center in the well-known resort town of Wildwood, New Jersey. All of this involved more than 550 volunteers at the local and state levels. Nate Zauber, New Jersey Pageant's executive director explains, "They do it because they know that Miss America originates in small towns like ours, and they enjoy being part of the system."

The winner of the state pageant in 1994, Jennifer Makris, received scholarships totaling $20,000; this figure accounts for her winnings at the local, state, and national pageants. Makris, a college student, says: "I went into the local pageant in November 1993, and competed in the State pageant in May 1994, and in the national pageant in September 1994. That's a long time to devote to the pageant, but the rewards are worth it."

When Robin Bobal goes to Mansfield to compete in the Ohio state pageant in June 1995, she will face thirty-six other contestants who also won their local pageants in 1994. (This number varies from one year to the next.) Jim Zellner, executive director of the Ohio State Pageant, travels to each one of the local pageants. "Putting together the state pageant and coordinating all the local pageants is a full-time job," he says.

The state pageant is held in Mansfield the third week in June, and local pageants for the following year begin just two weeks later. State preliminary competitions are lavish productions which are taped and then televised on local stations throughout the state, and the Miss Ohio Radio Network carries the event on twelve radio stations.

The city of Mansfield designates one week in June as "Miss Ohio Week," during which time festivities connected to or promoting the pageant are held. Sponsors are generous in Ohio — the state is ranked eighth in scholarships at the local level, and ninth in scholarship money awarded at the state level. Miss Ohio averages ninety-five paid appearances per year, excellent training for what's ahead of her in Atlantic City.

While the states are working hard to send their best representative to Atlantic City, the national office maintains its own year-round operation. Nothing changes in local and state pageants without first being decided by the board of directors in Atlantic City, and as national production manager, it is Bill Caligari's job to see that the information is passed on to every pageant office across the country. "Just think of me as a troubleshooter," Caligari says. "Whenever anyone in the system has a problem, they call us, and we work it out."

Without volunteers there would be no local pageants, no state pageants, and no nationally televised Miss America Pageant. The arithmetic is staggering — fifty states, some with as many as sixty pageants, can have up to twenty full-time volunteers, plus additional volunteers just on pageant nights — in all about 250,000 people. Nowhere is this more evident than in Atlantic City, where hundreds volunteer to help with the national competition.

Jayne Bray, chairman of the board of directors and press coordinator for Pageant activities, is a full time volunteer. "Not a week goes by when I'm not doing some kind of Pageant business. The press part starts in April and goes to October," she says. Most of the seventeen women who comprise the press committee have been involved with Miss America for many years. "They have established a very nice rapport with the press, they know how to minimize confusion and organize hundreds of interviews and briefings," Bray adds.

Contestants await crowning of Lea Mack, Miss Ohio, at the state Pageant in 1994 after a long week of rehearsals.

The other hat Bray wears — chairman of the board of directors — involves an additional investment of time and energy. Executive board officers meet every month and the full board meets every other month. The board approves all financial expenditures, sets policy, and makes major decisions. Whatever the Atlantic City board sets as standard is passed on to state boards of directors to insure continuity and compliance.

The only paid member of the board is CEO Leonard Horn. "When I assumed my current responsibilities back in 1987, I told the board that the days of a volunteer CEO were over. They gave me a mandate to bring the program into the 21st century, and I knew that was going to take a lot of work and a full-time commitment," he says.

When Lenora Slaughter enlisted the aid of the wife of Atlantic City's mayor to head the hostess committee back in 1937, she started a precedent that lasted for more than fifty years. Only the wives of socially prominent men were invited to join the committee, and for years it was an elite circle. As Ellen Plum, former head of the hostess committee remembers, "In 1963 when I was asked to volunteer, the main requirement was not one's credentials, but whom you were married to and what your position was in the community."

Volunteer hostess Audrey Fischer remembers that time as well. "Ever since I was a little girl I wanted to work with the Pageant, but I knew Jewish women were not invited to join.

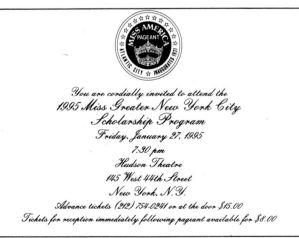

You are cordially invited to attend the
*1995 Miss Greater New York City
Scholarship Program*
Friday, January 27, 1995
7:30 pm
Hudson Theatre
145 West 44th Street
New York, N.Y.
Advance tickets (212) 754-0241 or at the door $15.00
Tickets for reception immediately following pageant available for $8.00

JUDI FORD
MISS AMERICA 1969

Judi Ford Nash was the first Miss America to compete in the talent competition as a gymnast. Her devotion to physical fitness for women continues to this day; she is an elementary physical education teacher and coaches the girls' golf, basketball, swim, and track teams on both the high school and junior high levels. Judi also manages to do some modeling and television commercials in the Quad-Cities area of Illinois and Iowa. She is mother to Brad and Brian Johnson who are in college, and stepmother to teenagers Drew, Molly, and Kelly Nash. Her husband, Jim Nash, is an attorney.

66

The scholarship I received as Miss America completely paid for my education, and gave me many opportunities that I otherwise might not have had. For instance, I served on the President's Council on Physical Fitness and Sports for eight years under Presidents Nixon and Ford. I believe the Pageant has endured because it reflects the changes in our country. When I competed, almost every contestant said she wanted to be a wife and mother first, then talked about career plans if she could arrange her life to do both. Today, contestants talk about careers and social issues and this change is reflected in the inclusion of the platform statement as part of the judging process.

99

L–R Bottom: Drew Nash, Brad Johnson, Kelly Nash. Top: Brian Johnson, husband Jim Nash, Judi Ford, Molly Nash.

miss america speaks

They opened up the committee in the late sixties and early seventies, and when I was first asked to join the committee, I declined. But then later I thought if the Pageant is making an effort to change, I should put my old feelings aside and pitch in." Now an eleven-year veteran, Fischer is glad she did. "It's part of Atlantic City history, and I grew up here," she says. "Besides, I enjoy being part of the Miss America family."

To understand the elitist nature of early hostess committees, one must remember that the Pageant was started by Atlantic City businessmen and hotel owners who lived in the surrounding affluent suburbs of Ventnor, Margate, Linwood, Brigantine, and Longport. In those areas, the country club was the center of social activities. The Pageant was founded at a time when women who could afford it did not work outside the home. Volunteerism was not only a social function, it was considered a civic duty. And among the choices available, the Miss America Pageant was a plum. It offered a touch of show business, a feeling of doing something worthwhile, a chance to be part of a national passion, and a bit of celebrity by association.

As in every area of its development, the Pageant's evolution in volunteer involvement reflects changes in society. Today, most volunteers are working women who put aside two weeks a year, usually using their vacation time, to work on the Pageant. "We now have a real cross section. We have women who work in supermarkets, we have lawyers, teachers, you name it. As long as someone lives within twenty-five miles of Atlantic City, and is willing to commit the required block of time, she is welcome," says Marilyn Feehan, head of the hostess committee.

The hostess committee has 200 members who divide their time during Pageant week working in one of the subcommittees. Some of the volunteers man the anchor station, the center of activity, where they answer phones, issue bulletins, and field inquiries. Fifty hostesses, working in shifts, accompany contestants on their daily schedules. Others are part of the transportation committee. And additional hostesses police the entrances to dressing rooms and rehearsal halls, screening the credentials of people attempting to get into those areas.

The food committee serves 8,000 meals during Pageant week. They solicit donations, arrange for the delivery of donated food, decorate the galley, set dozens of tables with fresh flowers, paper tablecloths, and paper dishes three times a day, and clean up after every meal. "I have a great sense of satisfaction and I enjoy the logistics of working out all the schedules. It's like a big puzzle," Feehan says.

Only one group of women involved with the Pageant do accept payment. They are the traveling companions required for each Miss America.

DEDICATED VOLUNTEERS

L–R Seated: Patti Lees, hostess volunteer, and Jayne Bray, national board of directors chairman and press coordinator for Pageant activities. Standing: Betty Chandler, Tessa Goldsmith, Barbara Greenberg, Marie Everleth, Jean Serber.

(L–R) Volunteer hostesses Bonnie Johns, Marie Nicholes, Marilyn Feehan, hostess committee chairman, Corinne Sparenberg, and Anne Frankel.

Jim Thornton at the Press Center during Pageant week in Atlantic City.

Miss America 1995 travel companions Michele Brennan and Bonnie Sirgany.

**Top: Miss Nebraska, Jennifer Love;
Miss Utah, Brooke Anderson; and
Miss Georgia, Andrea Krahn,
listen to last minute instructions
by Bill Caligari before the talent
competition in Atlantic City, 1994.**

**Above: Hostess Ellen Plum uses an
electric cart to get around in the
vast areas of Convention Center
during Pageant week.**

Mary Korey, now retired, was the Pageant's
first official traveling companion. "Before that,
Lenora or the girl's mother would go with
her," Korey remembers. "I was working at the
Atlantic City press bureau and took a leave of
absence," she says. "It was 1953, and my first
Miss America was Evelyn Ay, and my second
was Lee Meriwether."

Korey remembers being a surrogate
mother to the two young women. "I ordered
two pairs of shoes in every style and color
they needed, so if one pair was being repaired,
I had a spare pair. I saw that they took time to
eat properly, I answered their mail and phone
calls, I got them to their appointments on time, and I traveled 365 days a
year." Today Korey still corresponds with both Miss Americas and pictures of
Evelyn Ay and Lee Meriwether with their children and grandchildren adorn
the fireplace mantle in her home.

Ellie Ross, who retired as traveling companion in 1992 after serving fifteen
years, remembers the days when she traveled with Miss America. Times were
often hectic. Once a streaker appeared at the door of Debbye Turner's hotel
room. Another time she was caught in a hotel fire in Falls Church, Virginia,
with Carolyn Suzanne Sapp, Miss America 1992. And she'll never forget the
crash landing in the Greek Islands with Susan Perkins, Miss America 1978.

"I'll always have those wonderful memories," Ross says, adding with a
twinkle in her eye, "Just don't play 'There She Is' anywhere near me. I've heard
it hundreds of times, and I don't want to hear it again for a while."

Why do so many people from all over the country volunteer thousands of
hours to the pageant? "I call it 'pageant fever,'" Marilyn Feehan says. "We all
appreciate the opportunities the scholarship program offers to so many
young women." And Jayne Bray sums it up this way: "We all believe in the
system. We are a seventy-five year tradition and that makes it part of our
history. Besides, it's a wonderful feeling to know that you are part of the Miss
America family."

Behind the scenes in Atlantic City

National headquarters for the Miss America Organization are located in a large, square, yellow sandstone arcade building which faces Atlantic City's famous boardwalk. Inside this formidable structure, the Organization occupies a large space on the first floor. The front offices are adorned with huge studio portraits of every Miss America, and individual offices are decorated with favorite pictures from the Miss America scrapbook.

In this office, all major decisions are made, all press information is handled, the details of the yearly television show are coordinated, and the activities of the current Miss America are orchestrated.

In this hub of activity, Bill Caligari, national production manager, keeps the local, state, and national pageants working together as a cohesive unit. All biographical information, pictures of contestants, along with their talent video and audio tapes are sent here where the tapes are reviewed, timed, and, ultimately, cleared for broadcast. Here, too, the Pageant program book, sold to subscribers as well as on the boardwalk and at the door on Pageant nights, is designed and written. And a twenty-four page national field book entitled "Miss America In Review," created for the local and state pageants, is created within these walls. This field book, which includes a cover photograph of the current Miss America, forms a ready-made core of information for the local and state program books, and is sold to local and state pageants. They can then add local sponsor information, and pictures and information regarding their own contestants. The national program book is written in Atlantic City by Carol Plum-Ucci and Jim Thornton.

The national office also distributes a newsletter to all former Miss Americas and national contestants, to keep everyone up-to-date and informed. Major events in the contestant's lives, such as weddings, new babies, career changes, and outstanding achievements are duly noted, promoting the feeling that this is, after all, something of a family affair.

The general public can purchase Miss America tapes directly from the national office; Caligari and his staff maintain a tape and film library that dates back to the early 1920s.

Chapter Seven
Selecting Miss America

When something happens that seems to be unfair, rules change.

— BECKY KING
MISS AMERICA 1974

Points

THERE ARE THREE GIVENS in any Miss America Pageant: There is no conceivable way to "fix" the outcome; a lot of people will disagree with the choice; and the judging system works.

Starting in the twenties, when judges admittedly looked for "face and form," a point system was initiated that scored contestants on — gasp! — body parts.

In 1923, when the seventeen artist judges included Norman Rockwell, James Montgomery Flagg, and Howard Chandler Christy, there was a 100-point body breakdown that awarded fifteen points for "construction of head"; ten points each for eyes, facial expression, torso, legs, arms, hands, grace of bearing; and five points each for hair, mouth, and nose. When Lenora

Previous page: BeBe Shopp (top row eighth from left) remembers being judged in black and white striped cable knit suits which were not particularly flattering.

FACE AND FORM

Fay Lanphier, Miss America 1925, displays her face and form to her best advantage. In the early years, artist judges selected Miss America on "face and form" and scored contestants on individual body parts.

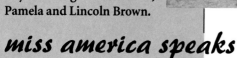
Slaughter began her association with the Pageant, one of the biggest prejudices she had to overcome was the filling of judges boxes with artists and illustrators who judged women on their measurements. It took ten years to break that stronghold.

In 1945, the year Bess Myerson won, the judges comprised an odd assortment of the traditional male artists and illustrators, women, and professionals from other fields.

Slaughter recognized that the modernization of the American woman, which was fostered by early feminists and nurtured during the war years, was going to be reflected in the new Miss America. She wanted to minimize the importance of actual physical measurements in favor of a generally well-proportioned figure and what she considered important characteristics. She instructed the judges for the 1945 Pageant to add new dimensions to their balloting by considering the following: beauty of face; voice, manner of speaking; wholesomeness, disposition, general culture; special talents; health, care of the body, dress.

That year Lenora Slaughter duly informed the judges that she didn't want a budding Hollywood starlet. She reminded them that this first scholarship winner must be a young woman whose poise and personality suited her for an advanced education.

The net effect was a board of judges predisposed to look for a winner who, besides being beautiful, could be trusted to make a good impression during public appearances and who actually had some real talent and some verifiable intelligence. Slaughter summed up her instructions to the judges this way: "Just pick me a lady."

Ever since those first years when Pageant rules were hastily rewritten to exclude married women, the rules and judging standards have continued to evolve and change.

The biggest change has been in the interview portion of the competition. Although interviews have been part of the proceedings from the beginning, it wasn't until 1936 that finalists were required to meet with the judges. (The category we know today as "interview" was once called "personality.")

"Interviews for Personality were held during two breakfasts, around tables, where judges moved from one table to another every fifteen minutes, talking and observing as they ate! It was a real challenge to try to talk and swallow at the same time!" BeBe Shopp, Miss America 1948 recalls.

Becky King remembers: "There were no points given for interview the year I competed. It was combined with evening gown. I felt I had won over the panel of judges on my interview and after I became Miss America, I worked hard to try to convince Pageant officials that the interview should have some points because that's where the contestant shows her ability to verbalize her beliefs. That's where she shows what she's made of."

When Leonard Horn came in as CEO it was with the foreboding that "if the Pageant didn't make some drastic changes, it would not survive." One of the first things he did was engage the services of a judging consultant to help clarify Pageant goals and structure the judging accordingly.

Leonard Hill, who serves the Pageant as a judging consultant, describes his role: "I conduct the formal orientation, first with the preliminary night judges, and then the Saturday night judges. I oversee the drafting of the process of the judging policy and rules and serve as a troubleshooter for their interpretation and then link the production process to the judging."

In other words, he tells the judges what to look for, and he works with the production team to see that writers, hosts, and contestants all know what to expect. He begins by telling the judges to view the Miss America contestant as one who is applying for a job, and that the four competitions are simply vehicles to learn more about who could hold that job. He reminds the judges that Miss America is going to be spending her year as a public relations representative. "Then I zero into the three key attributes to look for: that she be a role model, that's she's a woman of public interest, and that she be someone who can mobilize and inspire others."

Leonard Horn adds, "We promote the qualities and attributes of women today representing today's issues.

Bert Parks asks that all-important on-stage question in 1955.

Left: Contestants on the boardwalk in 1946. Actress Cloris Leachman is fourth from left.

SUSAN POWELL
MISS AMERICA 1981

Three of the preliminary judges in 1994. L–R: Nancy Gregory, Malcolm Poindexter, and Rebecca King.

LAUREL SCHAEFER
MISS AMERICA 1972

Laurel lives in Los Angeles where she
is pursuing a career as an actress and
spokesperson. She has performed in
many musical stage productions, and
has been featured in leading television
roles for a number of years. Laurel
began the Women's Leadership Foundation; this organization provides an
educational curriculum for teaching
leadership skills. She is involved with
the United Nations Unifam program
and attends international conferences
where she is often the facilitator of
topics concerning women.

*My mother was a widow when I was
in school, so money was hard to come
by. The Pageant scholarship gave me
the means to education, and education was the key to my destiny. For a
long time the negative aspect of being
Miss America was that professional
people prejudged me because of the
'beauty queen' image. The positive
impact of being Miss America was its
financial advantage. I am still
approached by companies for public
speaking engagements where being
Miss America helps sell tickets. I
believe the Pageant has endured
because it basically represents the
American idea that hard work can
bring success. The most extraordinary
change is the means by which Miss
America can get her message out in
the world through the apparatus of
The Miss America Organization.*

She is a woman with a presence, and she calls positive attention to herself,
with her talent, intelligence, health, and physical appearance. What the judges
are instructed to look for is the best composite; and that comes out of the four
competitions that we inherited.

"Another consideration we added to judging in the past few years is that
the judges select the young woman who best represents Miss America. That
adds a new dimension to the judging process, and we ask that question in
everything except talent on preliminary nights."

Inasmuch as the interview is now a major factor in determining the winner,
it is in that category that the most changes have been made over the years.

The on-stage question was dropped out of the final competition altogether
for a time in the seventies, then revived in the early eighties. No longer
frivolous in nature, the question was developed from issues discussed by the
contestant during her interview with the judges. Then, when the "platform"
requirement was introduced in 1989, each contestant was asked to write an
essay or platform statement. Today, on-stage questions are based on that essay.

When asked if that made it easier for contestants to answer the on-stage
question, Hill replied, "Now we try to find an aspect or dimension of the essay
that they will either have to analyze or take a position on, and that makes the
question writing very difficult. We don't want them to just start spilling out
their platform."

Over the years the Pageant has changed the focus of who Miss America is
by changing the number of points awarded in each category. BeBe Shopp
recalls that when she was a contestant, there were four categories: evening
gown, swimsuit, talent, and personal interview; and each received 25 percent
of the total points. Today the emphasis has changed, and competitions are
rated as follows: talent, 40 percent; interview, 30 percent; swimsuit, 15
percent; and evening wear, 15 percent.

Another major change has been in the way the swimsuit competition is
judged. BeBe Shopp says of the year she competed: "Swimsuits and evening
gowns were modeled individually, then in a group. We did one-quarter turns
in front of the judges with legs together on all turns. We had to wear Catalina
black-and-white striped cable knit suits which gave no support. We were not
allowed padding, glue, or tape, and we were checked. Compared to today,
things have changed a lot — and for the better!"

Miss America 1981, Susan Powell, who was a judge at the Pageant in 1994,
adds, "In my year we were not allowed to wear suits that were cut high on the
hip, and it was hard to find a suit because that was the style at the time. We
were not allowed to wear body makeup, and they checked our legs."

As a judge she had a different perspective. "That part is so subjective. As a
former contestant, I know that each contestant has achieved the highest level
of physical fitness that she can achieve for herself. For instance, there is no

**Laurel Schaefer and her "best friend,"
mother Eleanor Schaefer.**

miss america speaks

way someone who is short, as I am, can make herself tall for the Pageant no matter how much she tries. But she can stand tall, and she can exude confidence, and that counts," Powell says. "Another thing is we were told to ask ourselves if the contestant has the qualities and attributes to be Miss America, and that is determined during the interview. So the interview influences everything you see. If two contestants were equally striking in a swimsuit, I then voted for the one who had the better interview."

COLLEN HUTCHINS
MISS AMERICA 1952

Powell also explains that when judging evening wear, judges look for carriage and poise, and although they are not supposed to judge the actual gown the contestant wears (some can afford better gowns than others), judges take into consideration whether the girl has selected an outfit that's flattering and shows good judgment.

The criteria for judging talent also are subjective. Judges are asked to look for charisma, perseverance, and a good selection. "Say you get a ballet dancer and she's technically good, but she made a bad selection," says judging consultant Leonard Hill. "The music might be dull or the dance may be slow and sad. The point is, she doesn't connect with the audience. Then you might have a singer who is not technically great — don't forget they are very young and they haven't reached their potential yet — but she reaches over the footlights and grabs the audience. There's your talent winner." The same criteria apply to evening wear and swimsuit — that is, a contestant must command attention to herself in a positive manner.

From its inception until 1989, the Pageant was judged during the contestants' one week stay in Atlantic City by the same panel of judges. One of the most striking changes in the system has been to divide judges into two categories: preliminary night judges and Saturday night judges.

The preliminary night judges select the top fifteen contestants, ascribing a score from one to ten of the best composite of all phases of competition completed. The auditors then take this composite score, drop the high and low, and weight it by 40 percent. The ten contestants who receive the highest scores become the ten finalists. This score of 40 percent is carried over to the Saturday night competition.

"On Saturday, before the show, the new judges view video tapes of the top ten

TERRY MEEUWSEN
MISS AMERICA 1973

Terry and husband Andy Friedrich are the parents of three boys, Drew, J.P. and Tyler, and one daughter, Tory. Terry is co-host of "The 700 Club," and is also a recording artist and writer.

66

The Pageant afforded me wonderful employment opportunities in my field, increased my earning potential, and awarded me the money to continue my studies. The Pageant has endured because it has stayed relevant, and because it provides a platform for young women not found anywhere else. Its secret is that it continues to let the contestants be the focus of its energy. It has changed the most in its scoring process, but that has been a good change.

99

Terry Meeuwsen with family L–R: Husband Andy Friedrich, son Drew, daughter Tory, and sons Tyler and J.P.

finalists' interviews, but basically the Saturday night judges meet the top ten finalists the same time the audience does," Hill says.

On Saturday night, the contestants begin with the 40 percent score that has been carried over, then talent is awarded 20 percent, evening wear 15 percent, swimsuit 15 percent, and on-stage interview 10 percent.

After all those long months of preparation, after making it to the top ten and performing before millions on television, after the evening wear and swimsuit judging, it's all in the hands of the auditors who calculate all the scores and come up with the top five. And it's only the top five who have to endure that final test — the on-stage question. "We work with the network compliance people, the show's writer, and the Pageant and television producers to draft questions for the top ten," Hill says. "We write questions for all ten, and are prepared to go with five. That's where the final 10 percent comes in."

Today's Miss America must be an activist on an issue she deems important, a young woman who has thoughts of her own and is willing to use the celebrity of the crown to make a difference in the world. This change in emphasis is why the interview competition has increased in value and the other competitions have decreased.

The weighted value and the fact that the weighting shifts from the preliminary nights to the final night allows that the only way to fix the results would be to have every preliminary judge, every final judge, every auditor, everyone from network compliance, and the show's producers all to agree. "And that would be impossible," Hill says.

"There is too much at stake for us to risk everything to predetermine a winner. We have worked diligently over seventy-five years to maintain our integrity, reputation, and traditions," Leonard Horn adds. "We spend a great deal of time and effort every year to make sure our judging system is as fair and unbiased as it can possibly be. Today's judges typically include a wide variety of professional men and women — artists, dancers, musicians, educators, and writers.

The rewards of becoming Miss America extend far beyond the winner, with scholarships available to a variety of contestants regardless of the final outcome.

"There are no losers at the Miss America Pageant," Leonard Horn says. "It's like dropping a pebble into a lake and watching the circles expand and expand. When we select winners for all the various awards, we never know how many lives will be touched by those benefits. That's why judging is so important."

miss america speaks

Miss America 1986, Susan Akin, crowns Miss America 1987, Kellye Cash.

Scholarships

THE BENEFIT TO THE WINNER of the Miss America Pageant is obvious: In 1995, it includes a $40,000 first prize scholarship plus a year on the road with the potential of earning a great deal of money. With that there is celebrity, prestige, and the opportunity to expound a social platform. First Runner-Up receives $30,000; Second Runner-Up, $20,000; Third Runner-Up, $15,000; and Fourth Runner-Up, $10,000. Each of the five remaining finalists receive $8,000, while the other forty contestants each receive $3,000.

In addition, all preliminary talent winners in the 1995 Pageant will receive a $2,000 scholarship, and all preliminary swimsuit winners received $500. Including the local and state scholarship funds distributed in 1995, the Miss America Organization made available a total of $24,000,000 in scholarships in cash and tuition grants.

When Leonard Horn became CEO of the Miss America Organization, he expanded the opportunities for contestants to be recognized in special ways. With the cooperation of the program's sponsors, he helped develop special recognition for outstanding contestants. In 1995 these awards will consist of the following:

THE FRUIT OF THE LOOM QUALITY OF LIFE AWARD

WINNER · $10,000
FIRST RUNNER-UP · $2,000
SECOND RUNNER-UP · $1,000

Awarded to contestants who best demonstrate the value of volunteerism. The purpose of this scholarship fund is to recognize and draw attention to the value and importance of volunteerism in the United States and to expand involvement in community service causes throughout the country. More than $200,000 has been awarded since the inception of this scholarship program.

THE REMBRANDT AWARD FOR MENTORSHIP

WINNER · $5,000

Awarded to the contestant who made the most significant contribution to another person's life through her influence and guidance.

KONICA SCHOLARSHIP FOR THE VISUAL ARTS

WINNER · $5,000

Awarded to a contestant pursuing a career in the visual arts.

THE WATERFORD CRYSTAL AWARD

WINNER · $2,500

Contestants with a special commitment to study business management or a marketing-related field are eligible for this award. Waterford began its alliance with the Miss America Organization by contributing to the $25,000 Miss America-Waterford Scholarship for study at the new Miss America's college or university.

1995 THE MISS AMERICA WOMAN OF ACHIEVEMENT AWARD

WINNER · $25,000

Presented to the woman who most influenced Miss America in her year of service.

THE MISS AMERICA ORGANIZATION BAND SCHOLARSHIP

FIRST PRIZE · $4,000   SECOND PRIZE · $3,000   THIRD PRIZE · $2,000   FOURTH PRIZE · $1,000

Awarded to bands who march in the annual Miss America Boardwalk Parade.

THE BERNIE WAYNE SCHOLARSHIP FOR THE PERFORMING ARTS

WINNER · $2,500

Awarded to a contestant planning to pursue a career in the performing arts.

THE ALBERT A. MARKS JR. MEMORIAL FUND AWARD

WINNER · $2,500

Given in the memory of Albert A. Marks Jr. by the National Association of Miss America State Pageants to the non-finalist interview winner.

THE BERT PARKS AWARD

WINNERS · $1,000

Awarded to eight non-finalist talent winners.

Chapter Eight
Thirteen Days to Glory

Everything we do for the next thirteen days is done in the name of winning. It's like being trained for almost a year to go into battle, then winning the war in thirteen days.

— CULLEN JOHNSON
MISS VIRGINIA 1994

Rehearsals

Previous page: Contestants begin rehearsals on the stage for the first time at the Convention Center in Atlantic City.

ORGANIZATION, organization, organization. That's the key to gathering fifty young women, scores of parents, hostesses, traveling companions, state pageant representatives, television crews, members of the press, and national staff, and getting every one of them in the right place at the right time.

No general ever took his troops into battle with a more concise, detailed plan of action. Every minute the contestants are in Atlantic City is scheduled and detailed in a forty-two page booklet, which becomes the bible for everyone connected with production. In addition, the television production crew publishes a minute-to-minute schedule each day, while the press department publishes a daily list of events for use by the media.

THE WATERFORD CRYSTAL AWARD

Cullen Johnson, Miss Virginia, is the 1994 winner of The Waterford Crystal Award, given to the contestant with a special commitment to study business management or a marketing-related field.

Like troops assigned to different units, the contestants are divided into three groups: Mu, Alpha and Sigma. This arrangement was conceived by Lenora Slaughter in the early fifties in her struggle to overcome the hated "beauty queen" image. She hoped that using college sororities would help the public identify the contestants with something scholastic.

The selection of those particular letters was deliberate. The *M* of the Mu stands for "Miss," the *A* of Alpha stands for "America," and the *S* of Sigma stands for "Sorority." Thus, the contestants are members of the "Miss America Sorority." Lenora Slaughter's goal was "to see that every girl who wanted to go to college had a chance." So she inducted them into a college sorority as soon as they arrived in Atlantic City.

Coming from widely diverse areas, and not knowing what to expect from each other, it usually took a few days for the Atlantic City contestants to become comfortable together. That's why Leonard Horn decided the contestants should get to know each other before they arrived for the Pageant. Such a meeting, on neutral ground, would allow them to become acquainted, have fun, and relax. So in 1994, all fifty Miss America hopefuls met for four days in Disney World.

Day 1 · Monday, Sept. 5, 1994

Festooned with balloons and ribbons, the lobby of Convention Center in Atlantic City is organized pandemonium. A six-piece band plays old time music, while clowns weave in and out of the crowd. Photographers, hostesses, traveling companions, contestant's families, the press, television crews, and pageant staff mill around greeting each other and waiting for the contestants to arrive.

The fifty possible Miss Americas, flown in from Florida, are bussed from the airport in Atlantic City to Convention Center. At 11:00 A.M., the contestants are escorted to their places to rousing applause, and the opening ceremonies begin.

There are more officials than at a political fund raiser. Pageant and Convention Center officials, the mayor, councilman, assemblyman, heads of the hostess and press volunteers, and a score of security personnel crowd a dais at the far end of the lobby under a panoramic photo of Old Atlantic City, waiting to welcome the contestants.

Leonard Horn delivers an upbeat speech outlining the challenges ahead, concluding with a reminder that just being here is "something to remember for the rest of your life." Other officials give their own shorter, but equally inspirational welcomes, assuring the young women that they are "about to see how this city can make you feel warm and comfortable. A city that could keep the Pageant alive and well for 75 years. . . ."

During these introductory speeches, the contestants sit composed and patient, aware from this day forward their every gesture will be noted by someone. Though up since dawn, each young woman is perfectly made-up and coifed, that Miss America smile already captivating the crowd at hand.

What to wear in Atlantic City is always an issue. It is, after all,

Clockwise: Contestants arrive in Atlantic City from Florida.

Miss Montana, Yvonne Dehner, is welcomed at opening day ceremonies.

The Press Center looks confusing, but hostess volunteers are masters at organizing interviews.

The Galley at Convention Center is manned by volunteers. The food not only looks appetizing— it's delicious!

It is my pleasure to welcome you to Atlantic City. You have come here to represent your state in competition for the title of Miss America. Your presence here today means that you already have accomplished a great deal. It means you first have earned the confidence of your local and states organizations in having the credentials to represent them here. It means that you are a person of accomplishment and discipline — in essence, you are already a winner. It means you represent hope and challenge, and that you are prepared to be a role model for your generation.

We hope this is an experience you will remember for the rest of your life. We are all here to help you, to make your stay comfortable, accommodating, and, of course, memorable. We want you to remember Atlantic City as a high point in your life. But even more so, as a stepping stone to higher points in your future.

Good luck, have fun, enjoy your stay, and most of all . . . be proud. You are a winner.

— Leonard C. Horn

September; too late for summer clothes, too warm for fall clothes. For this first occasion, no one takes any chances. Most contestants are attired in office wear — demure suits with simple blouses, stockings, and high heels.

Amid the constant flash, flash, flash of cameras, each contestant is introduced, and each in turn is greeted with an equal burst of applause from the audience. Then, following the rigid printed schedule, at exactly 1:00 P.M., Horn wishes everyone good luck, and the first two hours in Atlantic City end. According to schedule, its on to the Press Center.

The Press Center is actually a curtained, partitioned area in a vast open space located next to the main arena at Convention Center. It contains about twenty round tables covered with pink tablecloths and small floral arrangements. At one end of the room is a large folding table draped in a colorful tablecloth and adorned with festive hospitality gift baskets.

Another partitioned area of this space is called the "Galley," where all food is served, and still another curtained area is referred to as the "Winners Circle," where special events take place.

The Press Center is a riot of confusion, with reporters and photgraphers jockeying for position, hostesses shepherding their charges, telephones ringing, and food being served.

A large map of the United States is displayed in the Press Center, a gift of the 1970 hostess committee. A cut-out of each state is prepared, and the girls' photographs taken as they sign their names on their state cut-out and place it in the appropriate place on the map.

As soon as a contestant has her picture taken at the map, she is escorted to one of the tables for interviews with local television crews and area newspapermen. After picture taking, interviews, and a quick lunch, the contestants travel by sorority group to begin wardrobe fittings. This continues in rotation until 6:30 P.M. when each contestant is escorted to her hotel by members of the hostess and transportation committees. Here her traveling companion takes over until the next day.

Cullen Johnson, who became accustomed to press conferences during her year as Miss Virginia, remembers "that first day it was like watching a movie. I felt I was not participating, I was just taking it all in as a spectator. Then someone called my name and I thought, 'hey that's me — I'm really here.'"

Day 2 · Tuesday, Sept. 6, 1994

At 8:00 A.M. sharp, all contestants are escorted to the Trump Plaza for a breakfast hosted by one of the Pageant's promotional partners, Waterford Crystal. At the informal buffet, a representative from

Choreographer Anita Mann greets the nervous contestants on the first day of rehearsal. The ladies will rehearse, rehearse, rehearse — then rehearse some more!

Waterford introduces the crystal scepter the new Miss America will carry on her winning walk down the runway, explaining that the crystal carving on top of the scepter symbolizes the crown, the orb beneath it represents worldwide fame, and the heart next to it represents the heart everyone puts into the Pageant.

Leonard Horn introduces Jeff Margolis, the television director, and his staff. Margolis assures the contestants that "this year will see the greatest Miss America Pageant we've ever had." He concludes, "We are here for you. The fact that you are here is what makes this occasion important." After breakfast the contestants report for a 10:00 A.M. rehearsal.

Instructed to wear red, white, or blue shorts at rehearsals which will take place every day for two weeks, and not trusting hotel laundry facilities, most contestants bring a new outfit for each day. Miss New York, Dione Robinson, says, "I had to buy fifteen pairs of red, white, or blue shorts to rehearse in — who else owns fifteen pairs of shorts?" "We all do," another contestant replies.

Anita Mann, the choreographer, has been working almost ten months on the show's production numbers. Her energy flows as freely as her long blonde hair, enthusiam evident in a smile as glorious of that of any contestant. Mann greets the somewhat nervous group of contestants: "Go to the bathroom before we start." The ice is broken; the girls relax and even allow themselves to giggle a little.

Mann has a Herculean task before her. She has to take fifty girls who have never worked together before, many of whom have little or no dance experience, and shape them into a cohesive dance troupe that will perform four perfectly coordinated production numbers in front of millions of television viewers. There are just six days until the first preliminary competition.

Mann looks down at the squiggly notes in her hands, the result of months of work with the musical director and assistant choreographer. She takes a deep breath and begins:

BECKY KING
MISS AMERICA 1974

Becky and husband George Dreman live in Colorado with young daughters Emily and Diana, where she is an attorney with the firm of Gottesfeld & Dreman.

❝

It was sometimes frustrating during my year to be used by people who didn't really know me as a person but were only interested in the name Miss America; but the positives outweigh all of that. The scholarship gave me the money to continue my studies — and the celebrity has always been fun. I think the Pageant has endured because it gives young people good role models. Also, all those thousands of grassroots volunteers are so strong and so committed to the program that it's going to take a catastrophic event to destroy that network! One of the most positive changes is the way Miss America was compensated during her year of travel. I was paid per day regardless of how many appearances I made, but today Miss America is paid for every appearance.

❞

Becky King, husband George Dreman, and daughters Diane and Emily.

miss america speaks

1920s

1964

What do contestants wear on the first day of registration? In the 1920s, they wore afternoon dresses or suits, and hats. In 1964, they wore afternoon dresses or suits, with hats and gloves. In 1994, they wore afternoon dresses or suits, but no gloves and no hats!

1994

"Think about posture, energy, use of arms. Feel the air, fill the space, don't slouch, pay attention, be aware of yourselves and your bodies." Before even attempting a dance step, she teaches the contestants how to stretch, how to relax muscles, and how to follow instructions. The audio man hits the playback button on his tape machine and Mann plunges in.

Rehearsal continues until 12:30 when everyone breaks for lunch and press interviews. At 2:00 P.M., the girls are divided into small groups where two assistant choreographers teach them the routines. While some of the contestants are rehearsing in these groups, others continue with their costume fittings. This continues until 6:00 P.M. when all contestants are dismissed from rehearsal. Day two is over.

Day 3 · Wednesday, Sept. 7, 1994

Contestants start the day with a 7:30 A.M. breakfast at Convention Center. Rehearsal begins in an upstairs ballroom exactly at 8:00 A.M. and continues until lunch and press interviews at noon. Then it's back to the rehearsal hall at 1:30 for more rehearsal until 6:00 P.M.

On this day a miracle unfolds. Fifty women who have never danced together before move in unison. What was mass confusion just two days earlier is now recognizable as the opening production number. Everyone is encouraged.

"I get my energy from the girls," says Anita Mann. "They are so enthusiastic, so fresh, so eager, I just can't let them down."

Contestants take time out to help build a house for "Habitat for Humanity."

Chevrolet, a proud sponsor of the Miss America Pageant, holds a photo shoot with the contestants.

Day three ends at 6:00 for all but seven of the contestants. At 7:30 P.M., after a quick supper, these seven compete for the Fruit of the Loom Award, a $10,000 scholarship awarded to a young woman who has volunteered her services to a specific cause during the year.

The finalists for this scholarship were chosen from those contestants who submitted essays to the award panel describing and defining their volunteer activities. In a small conference room at Convention Center, each of the seven contestants is questioned privately by a panel of judges about her volunteer activities.

Miss Idaho, Tracey Yarbrough, one of the seven, explains how she is able to redirect her energy after a strenuous twelve-hour day: "You can't lose your enthusiasm no matter how tired. After all, look where we are! At the Miss America Pageant! One gets tired, but the stakes are so high, you just psych yourself into keeping going." Yarbrough smiles, "You do it because of the goal you've set for yourself, and because you believe in what you are doing."

Day 4 · Thursday, Sept. 8, 1994

Day four begins as usual: breakfast at 7:30, rehearsal at 8:00, and lunch at noon, but then the schedule changes. On this day, five contestants who are finalists in the Rembrandt Scholarship competition are invited to a luncheon hosted by that Pageant sponsor. At 12:30, the forty-five remaining contestants board vans for a trip to an area of Atlantic City most tourists never see.

In a working class neighborhood of single wooden houses, Habitat for Humanity is building a house for a local resident. Homelessness is Miss America 1994, Kimberly Aiken's platform. The trip for this year's contestants is to publicize the activities of Habitat for Humanity.

While curious neighbors watch, the Miss America vans roll up and the contestants, wearing Habitat for Humanity tee shirts and shorts or jeans, plunge once more into the phalanx of photographers, video cameras, and reporters. Under a blazing sun, undaunted by the heat and humidity, protected by a cordon of security guards, they pick up hammers, shovels, and paint brushes and get to work.

The contestants seem unaware of the publicity opportunity this occasion represents. Miss North Dakota, Nicci Elkins says, "We're here to help build this house. We get our energy from knowing we are helping do something worthwhile."

Two hours later, the contestants are back in the rehearsal hall. They break for dinner at 6:00, then return at 7:30 to work hard until 9:30. It's been a long day.

Day 5 · Friday, Sept. 9, 1994

By day five, Mann knows every contestant's name and which contestants are the most talented dancers. She places these in front so the other girls can follow them. Friday follows the usual rehearsal schedule which begins at 8:00, breaks for lunch and press interviews at 12:00, and continues after lunch until 5:30. Then contestants report to the press center to end their day early with a Chevrolet photo shoot.

Day 6 · *Saturday, Sept. 10, 1994*

Unbelievably, it is just one week before the television show. While stage crews continue to set, light, build, paint, and install, the contestants walk onto the enormous stage in Convention Center for the very first time. This is the place where they will win or lose.

"My heart beat a little faster when I actually saw the stage of Convention Center for the first time. I couldn't wait to see the space," says Miss Vermont, Vanessa Lynn Branch. "You expect to feel really scared — but when I walked out I felt a sense of awe because this was the same stage Miss Americas have walked since the forties."

"It really hit me when I saw the runway," remarks Miss South Carolina, Kristie Greene. "It's a totally different perspective. I felt a cold chill because up to that time, being in Atlantic City had a summer camp feeling. Until I stepped on that stage — then it hit me — this is the real thing."

Facing the preliminary night judges alone for that all-important personal interview might be a little scary, but these young women are up to the challenge.

Actions speak louder than words: the body language from all of the contestants on this day says, "We're here! We're really here!" Rehearsal on stage continues until noon, and while most contestants go to the galley for lunch and interviews, six contestants go to the Boardwalk Mall to be photographed making fudge. A number of others have their pictures taken on the beaches of Atlantic City or publicity photos on the boardwalk. Everyone is back on-stage at 1:30.

The day heralds another milestone: the contestants meet the preliminary judges, a meeting that marks a major turning point in the countdown to the finals.

Three area girl scouts — Beth Ann Hall, Christine Jordan, and Allison Rohner — have each selected one Miss America contestant as mentor role models. They are Miss New Jersey, Jennifer Makris; Miss Texas, Arian Archer; and Miss Louisiana, Tiffany Mock.

There's an early dismissal, allowing contestants to return to their hotels to change into dinner dresses. At 7:30, all fifty contestants attend a mandatory charity dinner/dance at the Trump Plaza ballroom, a benefit for the Bacharach Rehabilitation Hospital located in nearby Pomoma, New Jersey. This is one more occasion to integrate the contestants into the life of their host city.

Day 7 · *Sunday, Sept. 11, 1994*

Day seven is the first day of personal interviews with the judges. Promptly at 8:30 A.M., the Mu 1 group reports to a conference room at the Trump Plaza Hotel. After nearly a week of group activities, the contestants must face the panel of preliminary judges alone. Each contestant gives a two-minute speech about her platform, then endures ten minutes of questions from the panel.

WEDNESDAY EVENING PRELIMINARY WINNERS
Swimsuit: Miss Alabama, Heather Whitestone
Talent: Miss Kansas, Trisha Schaffer

THURSDAY EVENING PRELIMINARY WINNERS
Talent: Miss Alabama, Heather Whitestone
Swimsuit: Miss Indiana, Tiffany Storm

FRUIT OF THE LOOM AWARD
L–R: Miss Ohio, Lea Mack (Second Runner-Up);
Miss America 1994, Kimberly Aiken; Miss
Arizona, Stacy Agren (winner); and Miss
Alabama, Heather Whitestone (First Runner-Up)

REMBRANDT AWARD
Miss Vermont, Vanessa Branch

Only one outsider is in the room: a television cameraman who is taping the proceedings. After the top ten are selected, their taped interviews will be shown to the Saturday night judges.

Miss South Carolina, Kristie Greene, is the first to face the judges: "At first I was terrified to learn I would be number one, but then I had a sense of relief. I felt that once the interview was over, I could concentrate on my talent. Not only that, but the first one sets the standard for scoring for the others, so I just set out to set the highest standard I could."

Miss Nevada, Laura Kim Hubach, the second contestant interviewed, says, "I was prepared to be terrified, but I actually found the interview fun. I used to be shy, and when I found myself standing before the judges, I knew I had come a long way."

Not even lunch today is restful. In addition to the daily press interviews, every contestant poses with the Variety Club poster boy, while three of the contestants visit with Girl Scout award winners. Meanwhile, a television crew interviews all the contestants for a planned documentary.

The day concludes with more rehearsals and a charity dinner and reception. At the end of the day, still in their rehearsal clothes, the contestants look fresh and energetic, upbeat, smiling, and patient. If they go back to their rooms and collapse with exhaustion, no one is the wiser.

Day 8 · Monday, Sept. 12, 1994

This is a repeat of the previous day, with contestants alternating personal interviews with lunch and press interviews. Rehearsal until 6:00 and the day is at an end.

Day 9 · Tuesday, Sept. 13, 1994

Another milestone. On this day contestants begin rehearsal of their individual talent on-stage. Tonight is the first preliminary competition.

First up on-stage is the Alpha 1 group, and the first contestant to rehearse is Miss California, Jennifer Hanson. "The enormity of it hits you. There you are on this huge stage, all alone. The music begins and you start. You get two chances to rehearse, and that's it. We're on that very night.

TUESDAY EVENING PRELIMINARY WINNERS
Swimsuit: Miss Virginia, Cullen Johnson
Talent: Miss Montana, Yvonne Dehner

CHERYL PREWITT
MISS AMERICA 1980

Cheryl lives in Tulsa, Oklahoma, where her husband Harry Salem is head of television with the Oral Roberts Ministry. They are the parents of Harry III, Roman, and Gabrielle. Today Cheryl travels full-time speaking, singing, and ministering all over the world, is a recording artist, and is the author of seven published books, with three more in the works.

66

Miss America gave me the opportunity to accomplish many of my goals through scholarships. I believe the Pageant has endured because it is the local contestants that make it what it is — the fact that any young woman from anywhere (including Choctaw County, Mississippi, my hometown) can win. The Pageant has progressed with the changes in the world, but its basic beliefs have not changed, and that makes it trustworthy.

99

Top: Cheryl Prewitt and husband Harry Salem with son Harry III, (bottom) son Roman and daughter Gabrielle.

miss america speaks

But we've trained a year for this, so nothing is going to stop us from doing what we came for. I just took a deep breath, and went on."

At 7:30, the house lights dim and the first preliminary show begins. As the professional dancers take their places, the two television cameras placed on the runway begin taping the show. The stage manager and choreographer huddle in a last minute conference. Backstage the contestants nervously line up for their entrance. On the other side of the curtain, a soprano sings our national anthem.

Suddenly, the curtain opens, the music begins, the contestants flood the stage, and the opening production number begins. One-by-one the women march bravely to the microphone, long hours of preparation providing the necessary poise, and announce their names. Then they each take their first walk down the runway — lights ablaze, waving to parents and friends, and smiling — always smiling.

Sixteen contestants from the Alpha group compete in the talent competition, eighteen contestants from Sigma compete in the swimsuit competition, and sixteen contestants from Mu compete in the evening wear competition and answer questions on their platform. It's a long program, but the audience is enthusiastic from beginning to end, applauding their favorites and cheering every contestant. Winners on Tuesday are Swimsuit: Miss Virginia, Talent: Miss Montana. Round one is over.

Day 10 · Wednesday, Sept. 14, 1994

Day ten repeats the previous day's schedule with a few special events thrown in. At 11:30 A.M., the Fruit of the Loom award is announced, and at noon the governor of New Jersey appears to lend her support.

The Wednesday night competition sees a renewed enthusiasm among the contestants. After the first night, the vastness of Convention Center is not quite so daunting. There's an extra lilt, an extra burst of energy, and the smiles (all fifty of them) seem brighter than ever. Tonight they sing out their names with more self-assurance. The dancing in the production numbers is tighter, more controlled. They sail through the first production number, then its on to swimsuit, talent, and evening wear. The winners: Swimsuit, Miss Alabama; Talent, Miss Kansas.

Day 11 · Thursday, Sept. 15, 1994

Today the TV cameras are "blocking" the show, so rehearsal on-stage is a lot of stop and start — and very tedious. In the morning, from 8:30 until 9:30, some contestants rehearse their talent, while those who already performed continue working on production numbers in the rehearsal hall.

At noon, all the contestants gather for a group photo wearing Waterford tee shirts, and at 12:30 the Waterford Crystal Award is announced. A crew from

Contestants rehearse with Regis Philbin and Kathie Lee Gifford.

"Entertainment Tonight," together with cameras from local television stations, tape and interview the contestants. The girls pose and smile, record a few sound bites, gulp down a quick lunch, and return to rehearsal.

At an informal buffet dinner, the contestants meet the show's hosts, Regis Philbin and Kathie Lee Gifford. The air is charged with renewed excitement; the contestants weave around the two stars, ask for autographs, chat, and try to relax. Miss Kentucky, Laura Sue Humphress tells reporters, "This is the first day I'm really tired, but meeting Regis and Kathie gives me new energy. It makes Saturday seem even more real. I feel that if I got this far, anything is possible."

Thursday night is the last preliminary performance. After tonight, the judges will select the top ten and end the hope of a crown for forty of the fifty contestants. None will know who make the top ten list until the big show, so all will embrace the stage on Saturday night with their dreams intact!

Thursday nights winners include Miss Alabama for Talent and Miss Indiana in Swimsuit.

Day 12 · Friday, Sept. 16, 1994

One day before the final night. Rehearsal begins promptly at 8:00 and ends at 4:00. By 5:00 P.M. the contestants are dressed to participate in the traditional Boardwalk Miss America Parade.

SUSAN POWELL
MISS AMERICA 1981

Married to opera singer David Parsons, Susan works in musical theater as a performer and actress. She lives in New York City where she also hosts "Home Matters" on the Discovery channel.

❝

The negative impact of wearing the crown is that sometimes it gets exhausting over-coming the preconceived ideas people have about Miss America. The benefit is that you always have an audience because people want to see Miss America. The personal benefits are tremendous. I used the scholarship to continue my voice studies and I really honed my craft during my year while on tour for sponsors. One of the reasons I think the Pageant has endured is because in America being the best and winning is everything, and everybody loves a winner! The platform issue has forced a major change because it encourages choosing someone who is willing to contribute her time and energy to a worthwhile cause.

❞

Susan Powell and husband David Parsons.

miss america speaks

One last rehearsal before the final competition begins.

Opposite: Miss America 1994, Kimberly Aiken, leads the Boardwalk Parade on Friday evening.

Day 13 · Saturday, Sept. 17, 1994

It's show time! Rehearsal begins promptly at 8:30 A.M., and is closed to all except the television and stage crews. Today belongs to perfecting the television show. Ready or not, at 9:00 P.M., live from Atlantic City, the show begins!

It's been a thirteen-day marathon; in two and one half-hours it will be all over and a new Miss America will walk the runway, glittering crystal scepter in hand and a sparkling crown atop her head.

Chapter Nine

After the Ball is Over

I have a once in a lifetime opportunity,
and I must use it to reach as many
young people as I can.

— LEANZA CORNETT
MISS AMERICA 1993

Appearances

Previous page: As the lights go out and the spectators go home, the day is just beginning for the new Miss America.

WHEN SIXTEEN-YEAR-OLD Margaret Gorman won the first Miss America crown in 1921, she took her Golden Mermaid and Silver Trophy, went home to Washington, D.C., completed her last year of high school, and that was that. From that time until the Pageant was discontinued in the late twenties, Miss America was virtually a one-night stand — there were no paid appearances for sponsors or civic organizations. Occasionally the winner capitalized on the title to further a theatrical career, but Pageant officials were not responsible for booking her performances.

In the thirties, the prize usually was accompanied by a few weeks' employment on the Steel Pier in Atlantic City, an offer of a Hollywood screen test, and perhaps a chance to tour with a vaudeville show.

O N   T H E   R O A D

Judi Ford and the Miss America U.S.O. Troupe entertain the troops in Vietnam
and other American military bases in 1969.

By the time Bess Myerson became the first scholarship winner, things had begun to change. During the forties, Miss America sold bonds, performed in shows for servicemen, and toured military hospitals. After the war, however, it was back to business as usual.

Immediately after winning the crown, Myerson made two appearances at the Steel Pier in Atlantic City, pocketed her two-hundred dollar fee, and went home to New York City. The respite would not last long.

At that time, the Pageant and the William Morris Agency had an agree-ment that made that agency Miss America's representative, and after only four days at home, Myerson was whisked away on a four-week tour of vaudeville houses in Newark, New York, Detroit, and Hartford.

"I hated coming out playing the piano in a bathing suit," Myerson recalls. "I had studied with a brilliant teacher since I was seven, I worked hard at perfecting my talent, I had already been playing concerts before the Pageant, and I was teaching piano. Then I was removed from a quality of life that had substance for me." While the Minneapolis Symphony asked her to appear as a soloist, and she performed with the New York Philharmonic Orchestra at Carnegie Hall, most of her non-vaudeville appearances were connected to sponsors of the scholarship program.

"The Joseph Bancroft people used me to model clothes for advertisements, and the Fitch shampoo people used me in advertising layouts in magazines, but since they already paid me by contributing to the scholarships, I received nothing more."

Myerson made appearances for the Victory Bond drive, visited the Senate, White House, and veteran's hospitals, and presented awards, but didn't receive monetary compensation of any kind — and her vaudeville money was running out. The Pageant arranged for paid appearances as well as for sponsor-related events, but except for the few Bancroft ads and Fitch layouts, Myerson was not getting any bookings.

"The years have diminished the importance of everything that happened that year, but I do remember that I felt rejected because Catalina didn't want me for their bathing suits, I was embarrassed when Fitch Shampoo placed an ad with me in True Confessions, and I was humiliated at appearing in vaude-ville," Myerson recalls.

"I was determined to do something meaningful with my year, so I began to travel across the country making speeches at schools with the theme, 'You can't hate and be beautiful.' I wanted to speak out against bigotry and racial prejudice of any kind, and eventually began to speak under the auspices of the Anti-Defamation League of the B'nai B'rith, and that has been a lifelong passion," she adds.

In 1945, Myerson didn't know she was starting something big. Yet, forty-five years later, official Miss America Organization policy dictated every Miss

America have a social-civic "platform" as a focus for her year of service.

Whether it was Evelyn Ay launching the 1954 Christmas Seal Sale or Lee Meriwether doing a benefit for a children's hospital in 1955, Miss Americas have had a tradition of combining their year with appearances for worthwhile causes.

Lee Meriwether recalls her year as Miss America: "As I had been the first Miss America crowned on television there were hundreds of requests to appear all over the country. There were four scholarship sponsors for whom I had to appear, and I crisscrossed the United States, Canada, and South America modeling in fashion shows, speaking at luncheons and dinners, riding in parades, touring children's and veteran's hospitals, interviews daily on radio and television, signing autographs, and appearing in store windows standing next to the television set Philco had named for Miss America."

Jacquelyn Mayer, Miss America 1963, recalls traveling through the country with media interviews, parades, pageants, speaking on behalf of sponsors, being seen at auto shows, modelling in fashion shows, in the United States and in London, and speaking for organizations like the United Fund.

Beginning in 1967, and continuing until the mid-eighties, The Miss America U.S.O. Troupe, which featured the reigning Miss America and six or eight outstanding contestants, toured Vietnam and other American military bases.

Phyllis George, Miss America 1971, remembers luncheons, conventions, sponsor appearances at factories and stores, parades, a trip to Vietnam with the U.S.O. Troupe, and local and state pageants. While Terry Meeuwsen, Miss America 1973, sang at churches and religious functions in between sponsor appearances, parades, interviews, and appearing at local and state pageants. She says she was grateful for the opportunity to "serve God" while traveling across the country.

Above: During her reign, Jean Bartel, Miss America 1943, was a vaudeville performer.

Top: Miss America 1945, Bess Myerson, hated playing the piano on the vaudeville circuit, but loved selling Victory Bonds on tour.

Above: BeBe Shopp toured for the Pageant sponsors.

Top: Miss America 1964, Donna Axum

Right: Miss America 1992, Carolyn Sapp appearing with Regis Philbin and Kathie Lee Gifford.

MARIAN McKNIGHT
MISS AMERICA 1957

Miss America 1988, Kaye Lani Rae Rafko, added something new. A registered nurse, she was a strong advocate of the hospice program and spoke on behalf of that program throughout her year. Inspired by her devotion, Leonard Horn began the platform program which is now an integral part of Miss America.

Debbye Turner, Miss America 1990, became the first to officially speak on her platform — Motivating Youth to Excellence — during her year of service. The following year, Marjorie Vincent took her message concerning domestic violence to people all across the country, and in 1992, Carolyn Sapp continued the tradition with her cause: education.

But it was Leanza Cornett, Miss America 1993, who really shook things up. Her cause was AIDS awareness. An outspoken advocate for the prevention, cure, and treatment of AIDS, Leanza was warned hers was not a popular subject, particularly for a Miss America. Cornett ignored the warnings, and with dogged determination took to the steps of Capitol Hill to help introduce the Comprehensive HIV Prevention Act of 1993.

Taking her message across the country, Cornett says, "It's not a closed-door issue anymore. It has to be open now because we're dying because of this. We're going to talk about sex."

Cornett combined civic appearances and sponsor functions with an unparalleled devotion to her cause. Her success in promoting AIDS awareness was Cornett's crowning achievement. She proved beyond all doubt that the platform issue was viable and worthwhile.

VONDA KAY VAN DYKE
MISS AMERICA 1965

Above: Miss America 1995, Heather Whitestone, on the road at Special Services School.

Right: Miss America 1990, Debbye Turner, at the Fayette School, Missouri.

Above and opposite page: Miss America 1994, Kimberly Aiken, whose platform was "Families First—Addressing America's Homeless Crisis," entertains children at a day care center.

Past Miss Americas have earned a great deal of money during their years of service; they are paid for every appearance, whether it be cutting ribbons at supermarkets or speaking to organizations. The question of payment for speaking about their causes has been raised by the media.

Karen Aarons addresses that issue. "Just as there are celebrities, such as sports figures and political figures, who are paid to speak on the behalf of causes, Miss America is also paid when she appears at benefits or conscious raising events. The sponsoring organization knows that her appearance will generate contributions, and Miss America's fee is part of their fund-raising expense."

"Remember, Miss America has no other income during her year. Her scholarship money must be used to further her education or to pay off school debts. If she chooses not to accept an honorarium for her appearance, that's her decision, but it's not the norm."

Considering the number of hours, the thousands of miles traveled, and the nonstop schedule, there is little doubt that any fee truly compensates Miss America. It is likely that her greatest compensation does, in fact, come from representation of a worthwhile cause.

GRETCHEN CARLSON
MISS AMERICA 1989

After finishing her year as Miss America, Gretchen Carlson went back to Stanford University to complete her undergraduate degree, and has been working as a television anchor/reporter since graduation.

"

Being Miss America has given me an opportunity to be a role model, developed my communication skills, and increased my self-confidence. I believe the Pageant has endured because it has changed as women have changed. Where once the Pageant may have been seen as the end-all for young women, today it is a springboard for young women. Also, while many Miss Americas have been involved with social and civic issues, today the Miss America Organization gives Miss America the support and means to get her message to a wide audience.

"

L–R: Dad, Lee Carlson, Gretchen Carlson, brother Mark, sister Kris, brother Bill and mother Karen.

miss america speaks

Dr. Debbye Turner finished veterinary school after her year as Miss America. She has been spokesperson for the "Caring for Pets" program sponsored by Ralston Purina, and now does promotional and educational work within the veterinary profession. She also speaks on youth and adult motivational communication and Christian beliefs, and hosts a series on pet care for PBS called "The Gentle Doctor."

66

Being Miss America changed my entire life! Everything I am doing today, and the success I enjoy today, was in some way facilitated by having been Miss America. I learned how to handle stress, crowds, and the media, and I had the opportunity to travel across the country and meet people from all walks of life. The Pageant has lasted so long quite simply because it represents all the best qualities of being American and the American dream. Biggest change? In my year we all had to walk the runway in swimsuits and high heels!

99

R–L: Debbye Turner with mother Gussie Turner and sister Suzette.

miss america speaks

The First 48 Hours

Sunday, Sept. 18, 1994

12:15 a.m.
Immediately after the telecast, Heather is escorted to the "Winner's Circle," where she catches her breath and is congratulated by Pageant officials who tell her what to expect next.

12:33 a.m.
Heather meets the press for the first time as Miss America. "I had to ask the photographers to stop flashing their lights for a few minutes so I could read the lips of people asking me questions," Heather explains.

12:42 a.m.
Minutes later, Heather is whisked away to her first official portrait session. She smiles radiantly as 75 pictures are taken in six minutes.

12:48 a.m.
Heather falls into her mother's arms, pride tacitly conveyed. The moment is short-lived as many other people wait to congratulate her, and in just 19 minutes she moves on.

1:07 a.m.
The other 49 contestants and their families welcome Heather at their party. "I love you all," she says, before moving on.

1:20 a.m.
Heather joins a party thrown for Pageant sponsors and judges at Trump Plaza, and mingles for a little more than one-half hour, greeting the many people who made this night possible.

1:53 a.m.
Heather returns to Harrahs, her host hotel to find she has been moved to the Presidential Suite. "I love being Miss America, so far," she says.

2:11 a.m.
Party number three is for family and friends in her magnificent suite.

3:30 a.m.
Bedtime! Heather falls asleep immediately, and "sleeps fast" because in four hours she has to be up, bright-eyed and ready to go!

9:00 a.m.
Heather's first day as Miss America begins with a media briefing by Miss America Organization officials.

10:00 a.m.
First press conference of the day. It goes off without a hitch.

10:30 a.m.
Presentation of car keys by Chevrolet. *Seventeen* magazine introduces "Beyond Beauty" essay winner.

11:00 a.m.
Return to TropWorld to change into shorts for beach photo.

11:35 a.m.
Another change of clothes for Chevrolet photo session. "I'm getting good at this," Heather says.

12:15 p.m.
Chevrolet photo shoot at the Carousel Room at TropWorld.

1:30 p.m.
Return to hotel and get packing. Enough of this Presidential Suite, now we're hitting the road!

2:00 p.m.
Pre-interview phone session with the "Today" show.

2:45 p.m.
Limo pick up for trip to New York City. "I could get to like this," Heather quips.

6:00 p.m.
At the Plaza Hotel in New York, another pre-interview telephone call, this one from the producers of the "Tonight Show."

7:00 p.m.
Dinner with Miss America Organization officials at the Oak Room at the Plaza.

9:00 p.m.
Wardrobe session in her Plaza suite.

Monday, Sept. 19, 1994

6:45 a.m.
Another limo. This time it's off to the "Today" show" studio at Rockefeller Center.

7:00 a.m.
Heather is a busy woman. While she waits in the "Today" show" green room, she participates in a pre-interview telephone session with the producers of "Live with Regis and Kathie Lee." Then it's off to makeup and hair.

7:35 a.m.
During her interview with Bryant Gumbel on the "Today" show, Heather dazzles everyone with her energy and enthusiasm.

7:45 a.m.
It's back in the limo for a short trip across town to "Live with Regis and Kathie Lee."

8:15 a.m.
While traffic made the trip longer than anticipated, there's still time for a makeup and hair touch-up.

9:00 a.m.
"Live with Regis and Kathie Lee." Heather is the first guest and is greeted with enthusiastic studio applause.

9:40 a.m.
By this time Heather is an old pro at climbing in and out of limousines and it's off to LaGuardia Airport.

11:42 a.m.
Flight to Las Vegas.

4:15 p.m.
"The Tonight Show with Jay Leno" pre-interview call at Heather's hotel in Las Vegas.

5:00 p.m.
Taping of interview for "The Tonight Show with Jay Leno."

10:15 p.m.
Heather flies back to the east coast. Changing time zones has her arriving at Newark Airport at 6:52 A.M., where

still another limo whisks her back to the Plaza Hotel where the next twenty-four hours begin.

As hectic as it might seem, that first forty-eight hours is representative of the kind of schedule Heather can expect on her year long tour. Miss America, Heather Whitestone, like those who came before her, will travel to all corners of the United States where she will bring her message to countless children and adults.

Beyond the Glory

Being Miss America is more than an honor. It's a job — with a rigorous, demanding schedule. Miss America is on duty 365 days a year, with the exception of a brief vacation during the Christmas season. Leanza Cornett, Miss America 1993, shares a four-month segment of her grueling schedule:

November 1992

Walk for Life '92, Florida
Teen AIDS Awareness Address, California
Future Farmers of America, Missouri
University of Indianapolis AIDS Benefit
Salvation Army Fund Raiser, Missouri
Project AIDS, Los Angeles Fund Raiser
Address Palm Springs, California, Chamber of Commerce
Visit Hospital in Michigan AIDS Wing
Macy's Thanksgiving Day Parade New York
World AIDS Day Kick-off, Washington, D.C.

December 1992

Broadway Cares/Equity Fights AIDS benefit, New York City
AmFar Benefit, New York City
Roche Labs Employee AIDS awareness week, New Jersey
Florida Institute of Technology
Child Welfare League of America, Washington, D.C.
Address, 4-H Club Chicago
Driving For Education, Florida schools
CenterOne AIDS Benefit, Florida
Arizona AIDS Benefit, Arizona
Address Health Care Conference, Florida

January 1993

Driving for Education address, Tennessee
NAMASP Conference, Louisiana
AIDS Tour, Michigan
Atlantic Market Center
Inaugural events, Washington, D.C.
NAMES quilt project, California
Superbowl event, California
Rogers High School AIDS Awareness, Michigan

February 1993

Boy Scouts of America Leadership benefit, Florida
NO/AIDS task force, New Orleans, Louisiana
UCLA/AIDS address, Los Angeles, California
Community AIDS awareness address, Norfolk, Virginia
AIDS Benefit/AZT tour, Greenville, North Carolina
University of Miami, Florida
AmFar Benefit, New York
Rotary AIDS lunch/University of Central Florida
Ryan White Youth Service Awards, Washington, D.C.

Top: Traveling companion Bonnie Sirgany, Mrs. George Bush, and Leanza Cornett

Children's Hospital, Denver, Colorado

Washington, D.C., The AIDS Quilt

Children's Hospital of Michigan

Addressing the Pan American Health Organization

LEANZA CORNETT
MISS AMERICA 1993

Chapter Ten
The Tradition Continues

Like America itself, The Miss America Organization is taking a bold look at the future and where we are going.

— JAYNE BRAY
Chairman
The Miss America Organization

Future

AT ONE TIME OR ANOTHER, Americans have celebrated politicians, war heroes, athletes, entertainers, and the very wealthy. For many years, this pool of celebrities was relatively small, dependent on public awareness of each individual's exploits through exposure in newspapers, books, or by word of mouth.

In the 1920s the instruments for democratizing and expanding popular culture were developed: movies, national magazines, radio, tabloids, wire services. The rise of mass media immediately generated a class of national celebrity — names and faces desperately needed to fill an ever-expanding media apparatus. Inevitably mass media reduced all celebrities, those who

KAYE LANI RAE RAFKO
MISS AMERICA 1988

Miss America 1988, Kaye Lani Rae Rafko, crowns Miss America 1989, Gretchen Carlson.

Opposite page: Miss America 1991, Marjorie Vincent, crowns Miss America 1992, Carolyn Sapp.

had achieved something as well as those who have achieved absolutely nothing, to the same level of notoriety.

Most people now regard celebrities as people who take to the national stage, do their act and leave, invited to return only when they have something new to perform. This permits many individuals a shot at fifteen minutes of fame, but it also virtually guarantees a short run.

And so it was with Miss America. Invented in the 1920s to sell newspapers and to enrich a little resort community on the Jersey shore, Miss America commanded national attention for a few days every September. She returned to Atlantic City one year later to shine briefly, only to be replaced with a new flame who faced the same short life.

The person who was Miss America did not capture our attention, only her persona did. Miss America became a celebrity, but as for the woman who was Miss America, few people could even remember her name the day after the telecast.

All that is changing. In the past, Miss America has endured as an icon of America's love of spectacle. Today, the woman who is Miss America is recognized as an individual who is pursuing her own ambitions. Today, the Miss America Organization is taking active steps towards redefining the role of the woman who is Miss America in a way that reflects American attitudes about women and societal values.

"This is an important crossroads for the organization. We want to seek out women who are going to make a difference in the next decade. We want the Miss America name to be used beyond the benefit of one contestant and we want people to think about her and follow her during her year, not just turn off the set and forget about her until the following September," says Leonard Horn.

"We have evolved beyond beauty and the Cinderella story. Today our audience cares about who Miss America the person is. They realize that she is a relevant role model who has the potential and the spotlight to help change some people's lives," he continues.

The Miss America Organization, in partnership with sponsors, has established scholarship funds for the college or university of the newly crowned Miss America. In addition, beginning in 1995, The Miss America Foundation will initiate a new scholarship program for economically disadvantaged teenagers. This scholarship will initially be awarded to one young

What are they doing now?

It isn't only Miss America who benefits from The Miss America Pageant. Throughout the years former contestants have used scholarship awards to help prepare for exciting careers. Here is a look at some former contestants

Dr. Sandra Adamson Fryhofer, husband George, and twins, Sandra Lynne and George IV.

**ELIZABETH BRUNNER RUSSELL
MISS ILLINOIS 1979**

Dr. Cheryl Hirst-Hodgins (right) with Cheryl Girr Mrozowsky, Miss Rhode Island 1966, at their 1994 reunion in Atlantic City.

SANDRA ADAMSON FRYHOFER, M.D.
MISS GEORGIA 1976

Dr. Sandra Adamson Fryhofer is a clinical instructor in Medicine at Emory University School of Medicine and has a private practice focusing on women's health. One of her proudest accomplishments was her election to the Board of Regents of the America College of Physicians. She is the first person under the age of forty, male or female, to be elected to this highly respected position and currently heads that organization's task force on women's health.

> *"I was able to use Miss America scholarship money to help pay for college as an undergraduate, and when I started medical school I was able to use scholarship funds from the Miss America Organization's Dr. David B. Allman Scholarship fund for medical studies to help defray the costs of medical school. Today, I'm in a position to have a direct impact on women's health, and that's more important to me than any criticism by those who don't understand the positive impact the Miss America Pageant has on so many young women."*

ELIZABETH BRUNNER RUSSELL
MISS ILLINOIS 1979

Liz Brunner anchors the NewsCenter 5 EyeOpener NewsCast from 5:00–7:00 A.M. on WCVB-TV Boston.

> *"I received $10,000 in scholarships while competing in local and state pageants, and an additional $10,000 from appearances during my year as state winner. That money helped pay for college. It takes a certain amount of drive to compete in pageants and I carried that drive over into my career. I didn't become Miss America — but I became part of the Miss America family, and that's terrific!"*

CHERYL HIRST-HODGINS
MISS RHODE ISLAND 1961

Cheryl is the mother of two children, and is a professor of social work at West Chester University in Pennsylvania. She is also a private therapist and is president of the Institute for Human Resources.

> *"As a psychologist and college educator I see a lot of young women who are so obsessed with their bodies that they often become bulimic or anorexic. For that reason I'm glad the Pageant has de-emphasized the beauty aspect of the Pageant, and would like to see the swimsuit competition eliminated altogether."*

CHARMAINE KOWALSKI RAPAPORT, M.D.
MISS PENNSYLVANIA 1978

Dr. Kowalski Rapaport is chief of the Post-Traumatic Stress Disorder Clinical Team at the James A. Haley Veterans Hospital in Tampa, Florida, and clinical assistant professor, Department of Psychiatry and Behavioral Medicine, University of South Florida, Tampa. She is also the mother of three sons. (The youngest was born in February 1995.)

"I was determined to become a doctor and entering pageants and essay contests was one way to supplement my income while studying. I recall crossing a picket line of women protesters at one of the local pageants and wanting to tell them I was competing because I believed women had the potential to be leaders and that I wanted an opportunity to pursue my chosen career. Today, I know I made the right decision. The nearly $20,000 I netted through competitions and appearances during my year helped enable my dream of becoming a doctor a reality."

DR. CHARMAINE KOWALSKI RAPAPORT
MISS PENNSYLVANIA 1978

MARY McGINNIS
MISS NEW JERSEY 1979

"The scholarship awards I received from competing in local pageants and the New Jersey State Pageant enabled me to earn a degree in music education, and I taught school after graduation. However, the visibility I received as Miss New Jersey brought offers from television stations, and I went on to study journalism at Temple University. I was an on-air anchor and reporter and assistant news editor at an NBC affiliate and am now the director of corporate community relations for The Miss America Organization.

"Since the platform became part of the Miss America agenda, I've learned a great deal by speaking on a daily basis with advocacy groups for issues such as AIDS, battered women, the homeless, and the handicapped. The greatest plus, however, is the privilege of being a woman who is in a position to help other women get ahead."

MARY McGINNIS
MISS NEW JERSEY 1979

DEBORAH RIECKS
MISS COLORADO 1989

"As Miss Colorado 1989, I became the spokesperson for Youth for Christ International, which has since branched off into the World Wide Leadership Council. That experience enabled me to travel all over the world.

"Being the Second Runner-Up to Miss America gave me the opportunity to pursue my life's dreams. Today I am pursuing a career as an actress and film producer. The competition process teaches one to risk being a dreamer, and since dreams don't always come true the way we envision, it's daring to dream in the first place that counts!"

DEBORAH RIECKS
MISS COLORADO 1989

woman in one state, though eventually it will be expanded to include one woman from every state.

Kimberly Aiken, who wore the crown in 1994, personifies the new Miss America. Her national speaking tour to assist in the fight against homelessness has given her great visibility as one woman who has used the celebrity of Miss America to make a difference. Her platform helped generate the formation of the non-contestant scholarship for economically disadvantaged teenagers — a program that will continue to benefit homeless girls across the country long after Aiken's year of service.

"The annual Miss America Pageant will always be an evening of entertainment, but it will also be increasingly competitive. The woman who wins the title Miss America must prove herself worthy of representing her generation of young Americans. As the future accelerates, the Miss America of tomorrow will be a very modern, openhearted young woman, ever more ready to tackle the political and personal challenges of our complicated contemporary lives," Horn explains.

Miss America, the icon, will continue to be a symbol of the women of her times. Miss America, the woman, will continue to espouse individuality bolstered by community spirit, self-awareness coupled with worldly knowledge, and proud femininity founded in independence and strength. Increasingly, Miss America will be the woman who best represents each of these long-standing American values.

Her celebrity will give her the opportunity, but her actions will insure Miss America's credibility, durability, and an earned admiration.

KIMBERLY AIKEN
MISS AMERICA 1994

We knew them when. . . did you?

These six Miss America hopefuls never achieved the crown, but they did have crowning achievements on stage and screen. Can you name them?

Clockwise: Cynthia Sikes, Miss Kansas 1972; Delta Burke, Miss Florida 1974; Vera Ralston Miles, Miss Kansas 1948, Joan Blondell, Miss Dallas 1926, Susan Anton, Miss California 1969; and Mary Hart, Miss South Dakota 1970.

KELLYE CASH
MISS AMERICA 1987

Chapter Eleven

Here She Is...

In September 1921, the first Miss America, Margaret Gorman, was crowned Miss America 1921. Miss America was titled according to the year she was crowned until 1950. At that time, Miss America's title referred to the following calendar year; Yolande Betbeze, who was crowned in September 1950, became Miss America 1951. This practice continues today, except for the fifty state representatives, whose titles still reflect the year in which they are crowned.

MARGARET GORMAN
MISS AMERICA 1921

RUTH MALCOMSON
MISS AMERICA 1924

MARY CATHERINE CAMPBELL
MISS AMERICA 1922–1923

LOIS DELANDER
MISS AMERICA 1927

FAY LANPHIER
MISS AMERICA 1925

NORMA SMALLWOOD
MISS AMERICA 1926

MARIAN BERGERON
MISS AMERICA 1933

HENRIETTA LEAVER
MISS AMERICA 1935

ROSE COYLE
MISS AMERICA 1936

BETTE COOPER
MISS AMERICA 1937

MARILYN MESEKE
MISS AMERICA 1938

PATRICIA DONNELLY
MISS AMERICA 1939

JO-CARROLL DENNISON
MISS AMERICA 1942

MARILYN BUFERD
MISS AMERICA 1946

BESS MYERSON
MISS AMERICA 1945

FRANCES BURKE
MISS AMERICA 1940

ROSEMARY LA PLANCHE
MISS AMERICA 1941

BARBARA JO WALKER
MISS AMERICA 1947

1940s

VENUS RAMEY
MISS AMERICA 1944

BEBE SHOPP
MISS AMERICA 1948

JACQUE MERCER
MISS AMERICA 1949

JEAN BARTEL
MISS AMERICA 1943

COLLEEN HUTCHINS
MISS AMERICA 1952

EVELYN AY
MISS AMERICA 1954

MARY ANN MOBLEY
MISS AMERICA 1959

SHARON KAY RITCHIE
MISS AMERICA 1956

YOLANDE BETBEZE
MISS AMERICA 1951

1950s

MARIAN McKNIGHT
MISS AMERICA 1957

MARILYN VAN DERBUR
MISS AMERICA 1958

NEVA JANE LANGLEY
MISS AMERICA 1953

LEE MERIWETHER
MISS AMERICA 1955

JACQUELYN MAYER
MISS AMERICA 1963

DONNA AXUM
MISS AMERICA 1964

MARIA FLETCHER
MISS AMERICA 1962

JUDITH FORD
MISS AMERICA 1969

VONDA KAY VAN DYKE
MISS AMERICA 1965

1960s

LYNDA MEAD
MISS AMERICA 1960

DEBORAH BRYANT
MISS AMERICA 1966

NANCY FLEMING
MISS AMERICA 1961

JANE JAYROE
MISS AMERICA 1967

DEBRA DENE BARNES
MISS AMERICA 1968

SUSAN PERKINS
MISS AMERICA 1978

DOROTHY BENHAM
MISS AMERICA 1977

TERRY MEEUWSEN
MISS AMERICA 1973

PHYLLIS GEORGE
MISS AMERICA 1971

KYLENE BARKER
MISS AMERICA 1979

1970s

PAMELA ELDRED
MISS AMERICA 1970

LAUREL LEA SCHAEFER
MISS AMERICA 1972

TAWNY GODIN
MISS AMERICA 1976

SHIRLEY COTHRAN
MISS AMERICA 1975

REBECCA KING
MISS AMERICA 1974

SUSAN POWELL
MISS AMERICA 1981

CHERYL PREWITT
MISS AMERICA 1980

KELLYE CASH
MISS AMERICA 1987

VANESSA WILLIAMS
MISS AMERICA 1984

DEBRA MAFFETT
MISS AMERICA 1983

ELIZABETH WARD
MISS AMERICA 1982

GRETCHEN CARLSON
MISS AMERICA 1989

SUZETTE CHARLES
MISS AMERICA 1984

KAYE LANI RAE RAFKO
MISS AMERICA 1988

SHARLENE WELLS
MISS AMERICA 1985

SUSAN AKIN
MISS AMERICA 1986

DEBBYE TURNER
MISS AMERICA 1990

MARJORIE VINCENT
MISS AMERICA 1991

CAROLYN SAPP
MISS AMERICA 1992

LEANZA CORNETT
MISS AMERICA 1993

HEATHER WHITESTONE
MISS AMERICA 1995

KIMBERLY AIKEN
MISS AMERICA 1994

Appendix

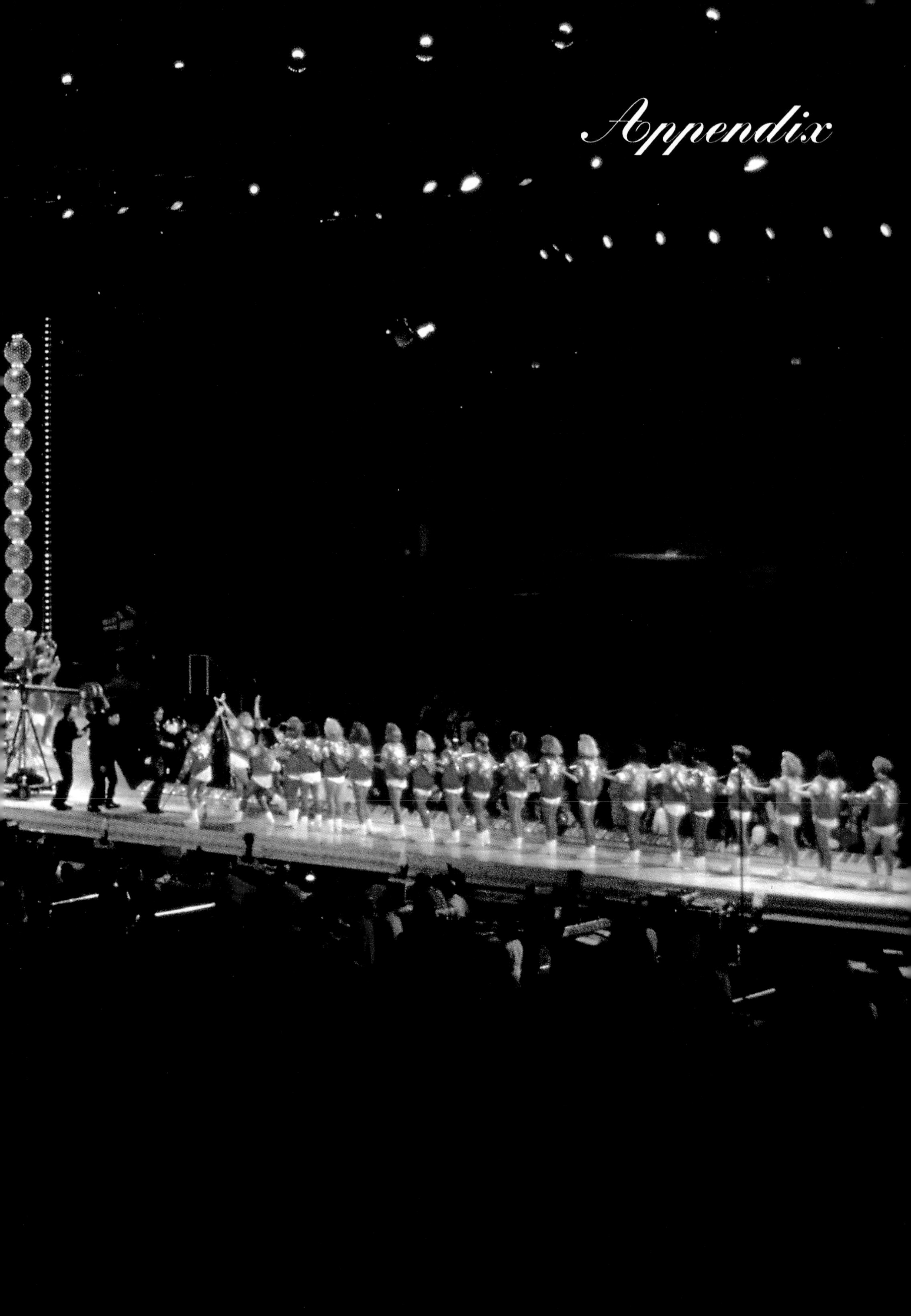

Miss Americas in Review

YEAR	MISS AMERICA	STATE	AGE	TALENT
1921	Margaret Gorman	DC	16	n/a
1922–1923	Mary Catherine Campbell	OH	16	n/a
1924	Ruth Malcomson	PA	18	n/a
1925	Fay Lanphier	CA	19	n/a
1926	Norma Smallwood	OK	18	n/a
1927	Lois Delander	IL	17	n/a
1933	Marian Bergeron	CT	15	n/a
1935	Henrietta Leaver	PA	17	Song/dance "Living in a Great Big Way"
1936	Rose Coyle	PA	22	Song/dance "I Can't Escape from You"/"Truckin'"
1937	Bette Cooper	NJ	18	Song "When the Poppies Bloom Again"
1938	Marilyn Meseke	OH	21	Dance "The World is Waiting for the Sunrise"
1939	Patricia Donnelly	MI	19	Song/bass fiddle "Ol' Man Mose"
1940	Frances Burke	PA	19	Song/dance "I Can't Love You Anymore"
1941	Rosemary LaPlanche College 2 years	CA	19	Dance
1942	Jo-Carroll Dennison Business College	TX	18	Song "Deep in the Heart of Texas"
1943	Jean Bartel UCLA	CA	19	Song "Night and Day"
1944	Venus Ramey	DC	19	Song/dance "Take It Easy"
1945	Bess Myerson Hunter College	NY	21	Piano/flute "Summertime"/Grieg's Piano "Concerto in A-Minor"
1946	Marilyn Buferd UCLA	CA	21	Monologue "Accent on Youth"
1947	Barbara Jo Walker Memphis State	TN	21	Song/piano/sketch and exhibit painting

1948	Bebe Shopp Manhattan School of Music	MN	18	Vibraharp "Caprice Viennese"
1949	Jacque Mercer Phoenix College	AZ	18	Dramatic performance "Romeo and Juliet"
1951	Yolande Betbeze University of Alabama	AL	21	Opera "Sempre Liberal/Caro Nome"
1952	Colleen Hutchins University of Utah/Brigham Young University	UT	25	Dramatic reading "Elizabeth the Queen"
1953	Neva Jane Langley Wesleyan Conservatory	GA	19	Piano "Toccata"
1954	Evelyn Ay University of Pennsylvania	PA	20	Dramatic reading "Leaves From My Grass-House"
1955	Lee Meriwether City College of San Francisco	CA	19	Dramatic monologue "Riders to the Sea"
1956	Sharon Ritchie Colorado Women's College	CO	18	Verse narrative "The Murder of Lidice"
1957	Marian McKnight Coker College	SC	19	Dramatic singing
1958	Marilyn Van Derbur University of Colorado	CO	20	Organ "Tea for Two/Tenderly"
1959	Mary Ann Mobley University of Mississippi	MS	21	Song/dance "Un Bel Di Vedremo"/ "There'll Be Some Changes Made"
1960	Lynda Mead University of Mississippi	MS	20	Dramatic monolgue "Schizophrenia"
1961	Nancy Fleming Michigan State University	MI	18	Fashion design show
1962	Maria Fletcher Vanderbilt University	NC	19	Jazz tap dance
1963	Jacquelyn Mayer Northwestern University	OH	20	Song "My Favorite Things"/ "Climb Every Mountain"
1964	Donna Axum University of Arkansas	AR	21	Song "Quando Me'n Vo"/ "I Love Paris"
1965	Vonda Kay Van Dyke Arizona State University	AZ	21	Ventriloquist/vocalist "Together"
1966	Deborah Bryant Christian College	KS	19	Monologue "Miserable Miserliness of Midas Moneybags"

Miss Americas in Review

Year	Name	State	Age	Talent
1967	Jane Jayroe Oklahoma City University	OK	19	Song/dance/conduct orchestra "One, Two, Three"
1968	Debra Barnes Kansas State College of Pittsburg	KS	20	Piano "Born Free"
1969	Judith Ford University of Illinois	IL	18	Acrobatic dance/trampoline exhibit
1970	Pam Eldred Mercy College of Detroit	MI	21	Ballet "Love Theme from Romeo and Juliet"
1971	Phyllis George Texas Christian University	TX	21	Piano "Raindrops Keep Fallin' on My Head"/"Promises, Promises"
1972	Laurel Lea Schaefer Ohio University	OH	22	Song "This Is My Beloved"
1973	Terry Meeuwsen St. Norbert College	WI	23	Song "He Touched Me"
1974	Rebecca King Colorado Women's College	CO	23	Song "If I Ruled the World"
1975	Shirley Cothran North Texas State University	TX	21	Flute "Bumble Boogie"/"Swingin' Shepard Blues"
1976	Tawny Godin Skidmore College	NY	18	Original piano "Images In Pastels"
1977	Dorothy Benham Macalester College	MN	20	Classical vocal "Adele's Laughing Song"
1978	Susan Perkins Miami University	OH	23	Song "Good Morning Heartache"
1979	Kylene Barker Virginia Polytechnic Institute and State University	VA	22	Gymnastics "Rocky"/"Feelin' So Good"
1980	Cheryl Prewitt Mississippi State University	MS	22	Song/piano "Don't Cry Out Loud"
1981	Susan Powell Oklahoma City University	OK	21	Classical vocal "Lucie's Aria"
1982	Elizabeth Ward University of Arkansas/ Arkansas Tech University	AR	20	Song "There'll Come A Time"
1983	Debra Sue Maffet Lamar University	CA	25	Song "Come In From the Rain"

1984	Vanessa Williams Syracuse University	NY	20	Song "Happy Days Are Here Again"
1984	Suzette Charles Temple University	NJ	20	Song "Kiss Me in the Rain"
1985	Sharlene Wells Brigham Young University	UT	20	Song/classical harp "Mis Noches Sin T"
1986	Susan Akin University of Mississippi	MS	21	Song "You're My World"
1987	Kellye Cash Memphis State University	TN	21	Song/piano "I'll Be Home"
1988	Kaye Lani Rae Rafko St. Vincent Medical Center/ Lourde College	MI	24	Hawaiian-Tahitian dance
1989	Gretchen Carlson Stanford University/ Oxford University	MN	22	Classical violin "Gypsy Airs"
1990	Debbye Turner University of Missouri, Columbia Veterinary School	MO	23	Marimba "Can Can"/"Flight of the Bumble Bee"/"Czardas"
1991	Marjorie Vincent DePaul University/ Duke University Law School	IL	25	Classical piano "Fantasie Impromptu" Op. 66 (Chopin)
1992	Carolyn Sapp Hawaii Pacific University	HI	24	Song "Ain't Misbehavin'"
1993	Leanza Cornett Rollins College/ Jacksonville University	FL	21	Song "A New Life"
1994	Kimberly Aiken University of South Carolina/ University of North Carolina	SC	18	Song "Summertime"
1995	Heather Whitestone Jacksonville State University	AL	21	Dance "Via Dolorosa"

States with the most Miss Americas

California	6
Ohio	5*
Pennsylvania	5
Michigan	4
Mississippi	4

*Mary Catherine Campbell from
Columbus, OH, won in 1922 and 1923

States with three Miss Americas
Colorado
Illinois
Minnesota
New York
Oklahoma
Texas

States with two Miss Americas
Alabama
Arizona
Arkansas
Kansas
New Jersey
South Carolina
Tennessee
Utah
Washington, D.C.

States with one Miss America
Connecticut
Florida
Georgia
Hawaii
Missouri
North Carolina
Virginia
Wisconsin

States with no Miss America
Alaska
Delaware
Idaho
Indiana
Iowa
Kentucky
Louisiana
Maine
Maryland
Massachusetts
Montana
Nebraska
Nevada
New Hampshire
New Mexico
North Dakota
Oregon
Rhode Island
South Dakota
Vermont
Washington
West Virginia
Wyoming

Miss Americas and their Courts

1921 Margaret Gorman, Washington, DC
1st Kathryn Gearon, Camden, NJ, amateur winner
1st Viginia Lee, New York City, NY, professional winner

1922 Mary Catherine Campbell, Columbus, OH, inter-city winner
Finalist Margaret Gorman, Miss America 1921
Finalist Dorothy Knapp, NY, professional winner

1923 Mary Catherine Campbell, Columbus, OH
1st Ethelda Kenvin, Brooklyn, NY
Finalist Heather Walker, Coney Island, NY
Finalist Marian Green, Philadelphia, PA
Finalist Charlotte Nash, St. Louis, MO

1924 Ruth Malcomson, Philadelphia, PA
1st Mary Catherine Campbell, Columbus, OH
Finalist Fay Lanphier, Santa Cruz, CA
Finalist Margaret Leigh, Chicago, IL
Finalist Beatrice Roberts, Manhattan, New York
Finalist Lillian Knight, Los Angeles, CA

1925 Fay Lanphier, CA
1st Adrienne Dore, Los Angeles, CA

1926 Norma Smallwood, Tulsa, OK
1st Marjorie Joosting, Washington, D.C.

1927 Lois Delander, IL
1st Mozelle Ransome, Dallas, TX
Finalist Kathleen Coyle, Philadelphia, PA
Finalist Virginia Howard, Tulsa, OK
Finalist Anne Howe, Hammond, IN

1933 Marian Bergeron, CT
1st Blanche McDonald, CA
2nd Florence Myers, NY
3rd Evangeline Glidwell, VA

1935 Henrietta Leaver, Pittsburgh, PA
1st Edna Smith, MO
2nd Jeane M. Megerle, KY

1936 Rose Coyle, Philadelphia, PA
1st Phyllis Dobson, CA
2nd Tillie Gray, CT
3rd Arlene Causey, Cook County, IL
4th Gloria Levings, Birmingham, AL

1937 Bette Cooper, Bertrand Island, NJ
1st Alice Emerick, Texas
2nd Ruth Covington, NC
3rd Phyllis Randall, CA
3rd Irmigard Dietel, Miami, FL (tie)

1938 Marilyn Meseke, OH
1st Claire James, CA
2nd Muriel La Von Goodspeed, UT
3rd Ruth Brady, Asbury Park, NJ
4th Gloria Smyley, Jacksonville, FL

1939 Patricia Donnelly, MI
1st Bettye Cornelia Averyt, OK
2nd Annamae Schoonover, WA
3rd Marguerita Shris, CA
4th Rose Marie Elliot, VA

1940 Frances Burke, Philadelphia, PA
1st Rosemary LaPlanche, CA
2nd Monnie Drake, MI
3rd Polly Connors, MA
4th Dorothy Slatten, KY

1941 Rosemary LaPlanche, CA
1st Roselle Marie Hannon, Western PA
2nd Jean Fidelis Cavanaugh, DC
3rd Lillian O'Donnell, Westchester County, NY
4th Joey Augusta Paxton, NC

1942 Jo-Carroll Dennison, TX
1st Bette Brunck, Chicago, IL
2nd Patricia Uline Hill, MI
3rd Madeline Layton, NJ
4th Lucille Lambert, CA

1943 Jean Bartel, CA
1st Muriel Smith, FL
2nd Helena Mack, Boston, MA
3rd Milena Mae Miller, NYC, NY
4th Dixie Lou Rafter, DC

1944 Venus Ramey, DC
1st Paulina McKevitt, Boston, MA
2nd Virginia Warlen, FL
3rd Elaine Steinbach, Chicago, IL
4th Betty Jane Rase, Birmingham, AL

1945 Bess Myerson, NYC, NY
1st Phyllis Mathis, San Diego, CA
2nd Frances Dorn, Birmingham, AL
3rd Virginia Freeland, FL
4th Arlene Anderson, MN

1946 Marilyn Buferd, CA
1st Rebecca McCall, AR
2nd Janey Miller, Atlanta, GA
3rd Marguerite McClelland, LA
4th Amelia Ohmart, UT

1947 Barbara Jo Walker, Memphis, TN
1st Elaine Mary Campbell, MN
2nd Margaret Marshall, Canada
3rd Peggy Jane Elder, AL
4th Laura Emery, CA

1948 Bebe Shopp, MN
1st Carol Held, WY
2nd Martha Ann Ingram, AL
3rd Vera Ralston, KS
4th Donna Jane Briggs, OK

1949 Jacque Mercer, AZ
1st Katherine Wright, MS
2nd Trudy Germi, IL
3rd Sylvia Canaday, CO
4th Jone Ann Pedersen, CA

Postdated

1951 Yolande Betbeze, AL
1st Irene O'Connor, SD
2nd Janet Ruth Crockett, FL
3rd Mary Jennings, AR
4th Louise O'Brien, OK

1952 Colleen Hutchins, UT
1st Carol Mitchell, IN
2nd Lu Long Osborn, NC
3rd Charlotte Simmen, AR
4th Mary Elizabeth Godwin, FL

1953 Neva Jane Langley, GA
1st Ann Marie Garnier, IN
2nd Jeanne Shores, CA
2nd Gwen Harmon, AL (tie)
4th Jo Hoppe, Chicago, IL

1954 Evelyn Margaret Ay, PA
1st Joan Cecilia Kaible, NYC, NY
2nd Anne Lee Ceglis, VA
3rd Virginia McDavid, AL
4th Susanne Dugger, MS

1955 Lee Ann Meriwether, CA
1st Ann Gloria Daniel, FL
2nd Polly Rankin Suber, SC
3rd Barbara Sue Nager, PA
4th Janice Hutton Somers, MI

1956 Sharon Kay Ritchie, CO
1st Dorothy Mae Johnson, OR
2nd Florence Gallagher, Chicago, IL
3rd Clara Faye Arnold, NC
4th Ann Campbell, OK

1957 Marian Ann McKnight, SC
1st Margo Zita Sandra Lucey, DC
2nd Anne Stuart Ariail, AL
3rd Barbara Hilgenberg, AZ
3rd Mary Ann McGrew, KS (tie)

1958 Marilyn Van Derbur, CO
1st Jody Shattuck, GA
2nd Mary Denner, OK
3rd Lorna Anderson, CA
4th Dorothy Steiner, FL

1959 Mary Ann Mobley, MS
1st Joanne MacDonald, IA
2nd Anita Bryant, OK
3rd Sandra Lee Jennings, CA
4th Betty Lane Evans, NC

1960 Lynda Mead, MS
1st Mary Alice Fox, WI
2nd Sharon Joyce Vaugh, WA
3rd Susan Bronson, CA
4th Patricia Anne Allebrand, AZ

1961 Nancy Ann Fleming, MI
1st Suzanne Marie Reamo, CA
2nd Ann Farrington Herring, NC
3rd Ruth Rea, DC
4th Tommye Lou Glaze, IN

1962 Maria Beale Fletcher, NC
1st Frances Jane Anderson, AR
2nd Carolyn Lasater, UT
3rd Linda Loftis, TX
4th Nancee Ann Parkinson, MN

1963 Jacquelyn Jeanne Mayer, OH
1st Joan Mary Engh, WI
2nd Penny Lee Rudd, TX
3rd Evelyn Keith Ellis, SC
4th Patricia Lei Anderson, HI

1964 Donna Axum, AR
1st Rosanne Tueller, DC
2nd Susan Dee Pickering, HI
3rd Martha Ellen Truett, TN
4th Susan Jean Bergstrom, AZ

1965 Vonda Kay Van Dyke, AZ
1st Karen Elizabeth Carlson, AR
2nd Ella Dee Kessel, WV
3rd Sharon McCauley, TX
4th Barbara Hasselberg, MN

1966 Deborah Irene Bryant, KS
1st Patricia Alice Puckett, MS
2nd Eileen Mary Smith, IN
3rd Carol Lynn Blum, FL
4th Sharon Mae Singstock, WI

1967 Jane Jayroe, OK
1st Charlene Diane Dallas, CA
2nd Vicki Lynn Hurd, TN
3rd Sharon Elaine Phillian, OH
4th Nancy Ann Naylor, NH

1968 Debra Dene Barnes, KS
1st Joan Myers, MS
2nd Barbara Baugh, WI
3rd Marilyn Cocozza, RI
4th Dawn Cashwell, FL

1969 Judith Anne Ford, IL
1st Catherine Monroe, MA
2nd Susan Alane Thompson, IA
3rd Marjean Kay Langley, OR
4th Katherine Field, IN

1970 Pamela Ann Eldred, MI
1st Kathy Lynn Baumann, OH
2nd Susan Anton, CA
2nd Cheryl Carter, NJ (tie)
3rd Judy Mendenhall, MN

1971 Phyllis George, TX
1st Claudia Turner, SC
2nd Karen Johnson, ME
3rd Chris McClamrock, MS
4th Maggie Walker, PA

1972 Laurel Lea Schaefer, OH
1st Karen Herd, ID
2nd Deborah O'Brien, MA
3rd Maureen Victoria Wimmer, PA
4th Allyn Warner, ME

1973 Terry Anne Meeuwsen, WI
1st Constance Anne Dorn, NC
2nd Linda Kay Olsen, PA
3rd Mae Beth Cormany, TX
4th Rebecca Sue Graham, IN

1974 Rebecca King, CO
1st Judy Hieke, WI
2nd Suzanne Plummer, NJ
3rd Debbie Ward, LA
4th Tina Thomas, PA

Miss Americas and their Courts

1975 Shirley Cothran, TX
1st Lucianne Buchanan, CA
2nd Jean Ahern, IL
3rd Darlene Compton, KY
4th Libby Lovejoy, LA

1976 Tawny Godin, NY
1st Susan Lawrence, NC
2nd Janet Jay Carr, CA
3rd Susan Kay Banks, OH
4th Stacey Peterson, AZ

1977 Dorothy Benham, MN
1st Lavinia Merle Cox, SC
2nd Carmen McCollum, TX
3rd Linda Michelle Mouron, CA
4th Sonja Beverly Anderson, NY

1978 Susan Perkins, OH
1st Barbara Mougin, IN
2nd Catherine Amelia Hinson, SC
3rd Mary D'Arcy, NJ
4th Cathy LaBelle, FL

1979 Kylene Barker, VA
1st Teresa Cheatham, AL
2nd Carolyn Cline, FL
3rd Sher Lynette Patrick, OH
4th Laurie Nelson, WA

1980 Cheryl Prewitt, MS
1st Tana Kay Carli, OH
2nd Michelle Elaine Whitson, KS
3rd Susan Wilson, MO
4th Marti Phillips, FL

1981 Susan Powell, OK
1st Paige Phillips, AL
2nd Donna Pope, MS
2nd Therese Hanley, NJ (tie)
3rd Lencola Sullivan, AR

1982 Elizabeth Ward, AR
1st Sandra Truitt, IL
2nd Krystal Ann Evans, GA
3rd Pamela Carlberg, IN
4th Sheri Ryman, TX

1983 Debra Sue Maffet, CA
1st Desiree Daniels, TN
2nd Dianne Evans, MS
3rd Yolanda Teresa Fernandez, AL
4th Nancy Chapman, OK

1984 Vanessa Williams, NY
1984 Suzette Charles, NJ
2nd Pam Battles, AL
3rd Wanda Gayle Geddie, MS
4th Pamela Helean Rigas, OH

1985 Sharlene Wells, UT
1st Melissa Bradley, OH
2nd Kathy Manning, MS
3rd Lauren Susan Green, MN
4th Tamara Hext, TX

1986 Susan Diane Akin, MS
1st Sherry Thrift, SC
2nd Jonna Fitzgerald, TX
3rd Honey Castro, WA
4th Angela Tower, AL

1987 Kellye Cash, TN
1st Julianne Smith, VA
2nd Dawn Elizabeth Smith, SC
3rd Kelly Garver, MI
4th Tamara Tungate, MO

1988 Kaye Lani Rae Rafko, MI
1st Patricia Brandt, LA
2nd Stacie James, NV
3rd LaTonya Hall, CO
4th Toni Seawright, MS

1989 Gretchen Carlson, MN
1st Maya Walker, CO
2nd Lori Lee Kelley, OK
3rd Marlise Ricardos, CA
4th Jenny Jackson, AL

1990 Debbye Turner, MO
1st Virginia Cha, MD
2nd Debbie Riecks, CO
3rd Jeri Lynn Zimmerman, IL
4th Kristin Huffman, OH

1991 Marjorie Judith Vincent, IL
1st Mary Waddell Gainey, SC
2nd Dana Brown, TN
3rd Suzanne Lawrence, TX
4th Linnea Marie Fayard, LA

1992 Carolyn Sapp, HI
1st Marisol Montalvo, NY
2nd Soncee Brown, MO
3rd Lisa Somodi, IA
4th Mary Allison Hurdle, MS

1993 Leanza Cornett, FL
1st Catherine Lemkau, IA
2nd Shelli Yoder, IN
3rd Pam McKelvy, KS
4th Du Sharme Carter, OK

1994 Kimberly Aiken, SC
1st Kara Martin, GA
2nd Titilayo Adedokun, OH
3rd Elizabeth Simmons, OR
4th Nancy Glisson, VA

1995 Heather Whitestone, AL
1st Cullen Johnson, VA
2nd Jennifer Makris, NJ
3rd Andrea Krahn, GA
4th Tiffany Storm, IN